The HOUSE PLANT EXPERT Dr. D. G. Hessayon
BOOK TWO

First edition: 100,000 copies

Published by Expert Books
a division of Transworld Publishers

A catalogue record for this book is available from the British Library

TRANSWORLD PUBLISHERS
61–63 Uxbridge Road, London W5 5SA
a division of the Random House Group Ltd

Distributed in the United States
by Sterling Publishing Co. Inc.,
387 Park Avenue South,
New York,
NY 10016-8810

EXPERT BOOKS

Contents

Reproduction by Spot On Digital Imaging Ltd, Gomm Road, High Wycombe, Bucks HP13 7DJ
Printed and bound by Mohn Media Mohndruck GmbH

ISBN 0 903505 61 4 © D.G.HESSAYON 2005

CHAPTER 1

HOUSE PLANTS
A–Z : CONTINUED

When looking at the plants that people have in their homes you could be excused for thinking that nothing much has changed since The House Plant Expert. But look a little closer at the plants in the various rooms and offices you visit — now you can see that there has indeed been a number of important changes during the past few years. Orchids were once admired by everyone but bought by only the few with conservatories and money to spare — now they are one of the most popular of all house plants. Joining them in nearly every house plant section at supermarkets, garden centres and DIY superstores is the peace lily Spathiphyllum. Its long glossy leaves and stately white flowers were once only occasionally seen in house plant displays, but now they are to be found everywhere. Chrysanthemums are now more dominant than ever in the temporary pot plant area, and both Kalanchoe and the Dracaena sold as lucky bamboo (page 119) have become firm favourites.

There have been winners and losers in the best-seller lists, but these are not the only changes. There is an increasing interest in Architectural Plants — the large specimens which make a definite statement in the room. These large specimens have broken the classical house plant purchasing pattern. The average customer has always been more likely to be in the 'mature' group than in the 'young person' or 'young married' class, but the position is now different when we consider the large container (4 litres and over) market. With these interior landscaping plants the young home owner has become the most important customer.

There are now exciting ideas about the way to use plants as interior design items and not just as green pets — you will find details in the Roomscaping chapter beginning on page 64. The result has been that our interest in house plants has increased — every year sales have gone up about 10 per cent, and one in three homes has plants in more than one or two rooms.

All this means that there have been many exciting changes since The House Plant Expert. See-through containers, decorative mulches and so on, but there is one key area which remains to be considered — the appearance of new plants in recent years.

The first chapter deals with 66 introductions which appeared in the late 1990s and the beginning of the 21st century. You will find Zamioculcas which is beloved by interior decorators and Anigozanthos which fascinates the young. You will find Curcuma at the DIY superstore and Pachira at the garden centre. As in The House Plant Expert these plants are classified into three groups. There are the Foliage House Plants which can be expected to live permanently under room conditions, provided their needs are met. The Flowering House Plants share this permanence, and the foliage remains after the flowers have faded. The Flowering Pot Plants are different — they provide a temporary floral display and are moved away or discarded once the flowering period is over.

Books remain the country's favourite source of information on house plants, and hopefully this sequel to The House Plant Expert will provide you with a number of new ideas to try in your home and a list of new plants to buy.

THE COMPLETE HOUSE PLANT INDEX

Acalypha hispida

Aphelandra squarrosa

Episcia cupreata

Hyacinthus orientalis

Grevillea banksii

Lisianthus russelianus

Platycerium bifurcatum

Plumbago auriculata

Pteris ensiformis Victoriae

Salpiglossis sinuata

Zantedeschia aethiopica

ADENIUM

FLOWERING HOUSE PLANT see page 3

Adenium obesum

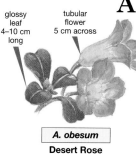

glossy leaf 4–10 cm long

tubular flower 5 cm across

A. obesum
Desert Rose

TYPES

The pink flowers of **Adenium obesum** are borne in small clusters on the stem tips — the variety **multiflorum** has pink-edged white flowers.

This summer-flowering tender succulent needs winter warmth, so it is not for everyone, but its large attractive flowers make it a welcome addition to the conservatory or sunny windowsill display. The bare stems have a cluster of leathery leaves at the top and a curiously-shaped tuber-like swelling at the base. A note of caution — all parts are poisonous.

SECRETS OF SUCCESS

Temperature: Warm in summer — at least 13°C in winter.
Light: Choose the sunniest spot available.
Water: Water regularly from spring to autumn but keep almost dry in winter.
Air Humidity: Misting is not necessary.
Repotting: Repot, if necessary, after flowering.
Propagation: Take stem cuttings in summer or sow seeds in spring.

ALBIZIA

FOLIAGE HOUSE PLANT see page 3

Albizia julibrissin

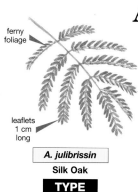

ferny foliage

leaflets 1 cm long

A. julibrissin
Silk Oak

TYPE

Albizia julibrissin is a slow-growing house plant with arching 30 cm long leaves which are divided into small leaflets.

The Silk Oak is an elegant specimen tree which will flourish in a bright and cool location. In its native habitat it bears pink flowers, but these do not appear on pot-grown plants. The long feathery leaves fall in winter, and they will also drop in summer if the room is too warm. Stand the pot outdoors in warm weather and prune the branches, as necessary, in winter.

SECRETS OF SUCCESS

Temperature: Cool — at least 3°C in winter.
Light: Brightly lit spot but shade from hot summer sun.
Water: Water regularly from spring to autumn. Water more sparingly in winter.
Air Humidity: Misting is not necessary.
Repotting: Repot, if necessary, in spring.
Propagation: Sow seeds in spring — keep at 20°C. Germination may take several months.

AMPELOPSIS

FOLIAGE HOUSE PLANT see page 3

Ampelopsis brevipedunculata variegata

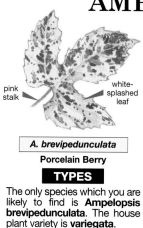

pink stalk

white-splashed leaf

A. brevipedunculata
Porcelain Berry

TYPES

The only species which you are likely to find is **Ampelopsis brevipedunculata**. The house plant variety is **variegata**.

The variety of this vine which is sold as a house plant is grown for its highly decorative leaves. It is deciduous, but the foliage remains for most of the year. Ampelopsis attaches itself to trellis screens etc by means of tendrils, and grows quite rapidly. Prune unwanted growth in spring, but any all-green shoots which appear must be removed immediately.

SECRETS OF SUCCESS

Temperature: Cool — at least 5°C in winter.
Light: Brightly lit spot — not direct sun.
Water: Water regularly from spring to autumn. Water more sparingly in winter.
Air Humidity: Misting is not necessary.
Repotting: Repot in spring.
Propagation: Layer by pegging down stems in compost during the growing season.

ANIGOZANTHOS

FLOWERING HOUSE PLANT
see page 3

green tubular flower segment

An Australian plant grown for its unusual flowers. In late spring the long flower stalks appear above the grassy foliage and each one bears woolly blooms with segments which have some resemblance to the paws of a Kangaroo. Despite its exotic appearance it does not need warm conditions — it should do well in a bright airy room.

A. manglesii
Kangaroo Paw

TYPES

Anigozanthos flavidus has 4 cm long flowers on 60 cm high stalks. **A. manglesii** has 8 cm long blooms which are bright red at the base.

SECRETS OF SUCCESS

Temperature: Cool or average warmth — at least 5°C in winter.
Light: Bright light with little or no direct sun.
Water: Water regularly from spring to autumn. Water more sparingly in winter. Do not use hard water.
Air Humidity: Misting is not necessary.
Repotting: Repot, if necessary, in early summer.
Propagation: Divide plant at repotting time.

Anigozanthos flavidus

APTENIA

FLOWERING HOUSE PLANT
see page 3

pink daisy-like flower

This tender relative of the garden Mesembryanthemum has become available as a house plant. It is a low-growing succulent with leaves which appear sugar-coated — it can be used to creep over and cover the edges of planters and other indoor gardens. During the summer months the tiny flowers appear among the leaves.

A. cordifolia variegata
Aptenia

TYPE

Aptenia cordifolia variegata is the only variety available and you may have to search to find one. Not spectacular, but it is a worthwhile novelty.

SECRETS OF SUCCESS

Temperature: Average warmth. Keep cool in winter — at least 7°C.
Light: Brightly lit spot — some direct sun.
Water: Water regularly from spring to autumn. Water sparingly in winter.
Air Humidity: Do not mist the leaves.
Repotting: Repot, if necessary, in spring.
Propagation: Take stem cuttings in spring.

Aptenia cordifolia variegata

ASCLEPIAS

FLOWERING HOUSE PLANT
see page 3

starry flower 2 cm across

This 50–90 cm tall shrub bears its heads of colourful blooms in summer and autumn above the dark green foliage. Each flower in the flat-headed cluster has bright orange petals and an inner yellow crown. Very attractive, but the plant sap is poisonous. It is easy to raise new plants from seed and some experts feel that it should be treated as an annual.

A. curassavica
Blood Flower

TYPE

Asclepias curassavica is the only species which can be grown as a house plant. There are others, but they are too demanding.

SECRETS OF SUCCESS

Temperature: Warm or average warmth — at least 10°C in winter.
Light: Brightly lit spot — some direct sun.
Water: Keep moist at all times during the growing season. Water more sparingly in winter.
Air Humidity: Mist leaves occasionally.
Repotting: Repot, if necessary, in spring.
Propagation: Sow seeds in early spring.

Asclepias curassavica

CAESALPINIA

FLOWERING HOUSE PLANT see page 3

erect flower-head up to 30 cm high

C. gilliesii
Bird of Paradise

TYPES

Caesalpinia gilliesii is the species which is usually offered — each flower-head bears about 30 flowers. **C. japonica** is similar.

This showy shrub belongs in the conservatory rather than the living room, although you might find it on the house plant table at the garden centre. It is a tall-growing plant which is kept in check by annual pruning. The ferny leaves are about 20 cm long and the flower-heads appear in summer. The 10 cm long red stamens are an eye-catching feature.

SECRETS OF SUCCESS

Temperature: Average warmth — at least 5°C in winter.
Light: Brightly lit spot — some direct sun.
Water: Water regularly from spring to autumn. Water more sparingly in winter.
Air Humidity: Mist leaves occasionally.
Repotting: Repot, if necessary, in spring.
Propagation: Take stem cuttings in summer or sow seeds in spring.

Caesalpinia gilliesii

CASSIA

FLOWERING HOUSE PLANT see page 3

flower 2 cm across

C. corymbosa
Cassia

TYPES

Several species, such as **Cassia didymobotrya**, are grown indoors, but **C. corymbosa** is the only one you are likely to find.

Masses of 10 cm wide flower-heads are borne above the foliage of this spreading evergreen shrub in summer or early autumn. Each cluster bears 10–20 golden flowers and the long leaves are divided into several pale green, lance-shaped leaflets. An attractive plant, but remember that this member of the bean family is poisonous.

SECRETS OF SUCCESS

Temperature: Average warmth — at least 5°C in winter.
Light: Brightly lit spot — some direct sun.
Water: Keep moist at all times during the growing season. Water more sparingly in winter.
Air Humidity: Mist leaves occasionally.
Repotting: Repot, if necessary, in spring.
Propagation: Take stem cuttings in summer or sow seeds in spring.

Cassia corymbosa

CHAMAELAUCIUM

FLOWERING HOUSE PLANT see page 3

flower 1 cm across

leaf 3 cm long

C. uncinatum
Chamaelaucium

TYPES

Chamaelaucium uncinatum is the basic species — there are purple (**'Purple Pride'**), pink (**'Bundara Excelsior'**) and white (**album**) varieties.

An evergreen conservatory shrub which has started to move inside as a house plant. The wiry stems bear narrow leaves which are triangular in cross section and sharply pointed at the tip. In late spring or summer the 5-petalled flowers appear in terminal clusters — each bloom is cupped at the centre. Prune stems after flowering to keep growth in check.

SECRETS OF SUCCESS

Temperature: Warm or average warmth — at least 5°C in winter.
Light: Brightly lit spot — some direct sun.
Water: Keep moist at all times during the growing season. Water more sparingly in winter.
Air Humidity: Mist leaves occasionally.
Repotting: Repot, if necessary, in spring.
Propagation: Take stem cuttings in summer.

Chamaelaucium uncinatum

CLUSIA

FOLIAGE HOUSE PLANT *see page 3*

shiny leaf 20 cm long

A rarity from S. America which can be used as a bold specimen plant. It grows slowly and the large oval leaves have a rubber plant appearance. In its native home it grows on trees and rocks and produces pink Camellia-like flowers followed by small fruits, but these do not appear when it is grown as a house plant.

C. rosea

Autograph Tree

TYPES

The usual species is **Clusia rosea** — a variegated type (**marginata**) is available. A free-draining compost is necessary.

SECRETS OF SUCCESS

Temperature: Warm in summer — at least 18°C in winter.
Light: Lightly shaded spot — avoid direct sun.
Water: Water regularly from spring to autumn. Water more sparingly in winter.
Air Humidity: Mist leaves frequently.
Repotting: Repot in spring.
Propagation: Take stem cuttings in summer or layer shoots in spring.

Clusia rosea

COBAEA

FLOWERING HOUSE PLANT *see page 3*

flower 8 cm long

The Cup and Saucer Vine is grown outdoors as an annual, but indoors it is a rampant perennial climber. It can be used for screening in the living room, but is more at home on the wall of a conservatory. The bell-shaped flowers (purple cup and pale green saucer) appear from midsummer to autumn — cut back hard once flowering has finished.

C. scandens

Cup and Saucer Vine

TYPES

The basic species is **Cobaea scandens** and there are several varieties with cups in various colours — **alba** is yellowish-green.

SECRETS OF SUCCESS

Temperature: Cool or average warmth — keep cool but frost-free in winter.
Light: Brightly lit spot or light shade.
Water: Water regularly from spring to autumn. Water more sparingly in winter.
Air Humidity: Mist leaves occasionally.
Repotting: Repot, if necessary, in spring.
Propagation: Sow seeds in spring.

Cobaea scandens

CODONANTHE

FLOWERING HOUSE PLANT *see page 3*

flower 1 cm long

This unusual plant is related to Columnea and shares the family growth habit of trailing stems dotted with flowers. Use it in a hanging basket or grow on a pedestal — turn the pot to ensure even growth. The leaves are lance-shaped and the waxy blooms which appear in late spring and summer are followed by red berries.

C. gracilis

Codonanthe

TYPES

Codonanthe gracilis is the most popular species — the tubular flowers are white with a coloured throat. Other species have pink or spotted blooms.

SECRETS OF SUCCESS

Temperature: Warm or average warmth — at least 13°C in winter.
Light: Brightly lit spot or light shade — no direct sun.
Water: Water regularly from spring to autumn. Water more sparingly in winter.
Air Humidity: Mist leaves occasionally.
Repotting: Repot every year in spring.
Propagation: Take stem cuttings in spring.

Codonanthe gracilis

COPROSMA

FOLIAGE HOUSE PLANT
see page 3

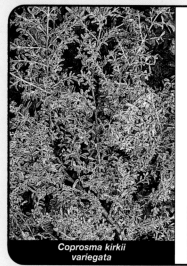

Coprosma comes in a range of growth habits, leaf shapes and colours. The plant may be upright, bushy or trailing and the all-green or variegated leaves may be rounded or strap-shaped. The flowers are inconspicuous and you will have to grow a male and female plant if you want to have berries. The variegated trailers are the ones to choose.

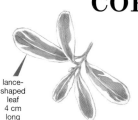

lance-shaped leaf 4 cm long

C. kirkii variegata
Coprosma

TYPES

Coprosma kirkii variegata is the most popular one — the leaves have white margins. **C. 'Beatson's Gold'** has yellow-splashed leaves.

Coprosma kirkii variegata

SECRETS OF SUCCESS

Temperature: Cool — at least 5°C in winter.
Light: Brightly lit spot — some direct sun is acceptable.
Water: Water regularly from spring to autumn. Water more sparingly in winter.
Air Humidity: Misting is not necessary.
Repotting: Repot, if necessary, in spring.
Propagation: Take stem cuttings in late summer or sow seeds in spring.

CORREA

FLOWERING HOUSE PLANT
see page 3

Here is one to grow if you like something new. This evergreen shrubby plant has oval leaves and the pendent tubular flowers appear in spring. There are numerous varieties available from house plant nurseries, and you may find one at your garden centre. Not difficult to grow, but use lime-free water and ericaceous compost when repotting.

flower 3 cm long borne in small cluster

C. 'Dusky Bells'
Australian Fuchsia

TYPES

Correa 'Dusky Bells' (30–60 cm) is one of the smaller varieties — **C. backhousiana** (white) and **C. reflexa** (white-mouthed red flowers) are taller.

Correa 'Dusky Bells'

SECRETS OF SUCCESS

Temperature: Cool or average warmth — at least 5°C in winter.
Light: Brightly lit spot — some direct sun is acceptable.
Water: Water regularly from spring to autumn. Water more sparingly in winter.
Air Humidity: Mist leaves occasionally.
Repotting: Repot every year in spring.
Propagation: Take stem cuttings in spring.

CORYNOCARPUS

FOLIAGE HOUSE PLANT
see page 3

A large focal-point plant from New Zealand — a good choice where there is plenty of room. The leaves are the key feature — leathery, glossy green and shiny. The small summer flowers develop into yellow-orange fruits with poisonous seeds. Left unpruned Corynocarpus will reach 2 m or more — young plants may require staking.

leaf 10–20 cm long

C. laevigatus
Karaka Laurel

TYPES

Corynocarpus laevigatus is the basic species. There are more colourful varieties — look for **albovariegatus** or **variegatus.**

Corynocarpus laevigatus albovariegatus

SECRETS OF SUCCESS

Temperature: Cool or average warmth — at least 5°C in winter.
Light: Brightly lit spot, but shade from hot summer sun.
Water: Water regularly from spring to autumn. Water more sparingly in winter.
Air Humidity: Misting is not necessary.
Repotting: Repot, if necessary, in spring.
Propagation: Take stem cuttings in summer.

CURCUMA

FLOWERING POT PLANT
see page 3

Curcuma alismatifolia

flower-head 15 cm high

C. roscoeana

Curcuma

TYPES

The bracts of **Curcuma roscoeana** turn from green to orange or orange-red. There are smaller-headed ones — e.g **C. alismatifolia**.

This showy member of the ginger family appeared in the garden centres during the 1990s. The leaves arise directly out of the compost and in summer the flower-heads appear. These are made up of overlapping colourful bracts. Watering stops in autumn, and in spring the fleshy rhizome is removed and repotted and then watering starts again.

SECRETS OF SUCCESS

Temperature: Warm or average warmth — at least 15°C in winter.
Light: Brightly lit spot but shade from hot summer sun.
Water: Water regularly from spring to late summer. Do not water during resting period.
Air Humidity: Mist leaves frequently.
Repotting: Repot every year in spring.
Propagation: Divide rhizome when repotting.

ECHIUM

FLOWERING HOUSE PLANT
see page 3

Echium fastuosum

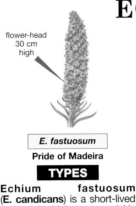
flower-head 30 cm high

E. fastuosum

Pride of Madeira

TYPES

Echium fastuosum (E. candicans) is a short-lived perennial which grows quickly and needs a lot of space. White and blue varieties are available.

The bedding plant E. plantagineum can be grown in pots as a flowering pot plant for temporary display, but for a more permanent house plant it is necessary to choose the shrubby tender species. The lance-shaped leaves are downy and the small flowers are crowded on cone-shaped heads which appear in spring or summer.

SECRETS OF SUCCESS

Temperature: Cool — at least 5°C in winter.
Light: Brightly lit spot — some direct sun is acceptable.
Water: Water regularly from spring to autumn. Water more sparingly in winter.
Air Humidity: Mist leaves occasionally.
Repotting: Repot, if necessary, in spring.
Propagation: Take stem cuttings in summer or sow seeds in spring.

ELETTARIA

FOLIAGE HOUSE PLANT
see page 3

Elettaria cardamomum

glossy leaf — silky underneath 30–60 cm long

E. cardamomum

Cardamon

TYPE

Elettaria cardamomum is the only species sold for indoor cultivation — best in a conservatory. Bruised leaves have a spicy aroma.

There are many popular house plants grown for their foliage which have large leaves that sheathe the stems — Aglaonema, Dracaena etc. This one is available from specialist nurseries and can produce a 2 m tall shrub if left unpruned. The white flowers and seeds (the source of the spice cardamon) are not produced on plants grown in pots.

SECRETS OF SUCCESS

Temperature: Warm or average warmth. Keep cool in winter (13°–16°C).
Light: Brightly lit spot — not direct sun.
Water: Water regularly from spring to autumn. Water more sparingly in winter.
Air Humidity: Mist leaves occasionally.
Repotting: Repot, if necessary, in spring.
Propagation: Divide plant at repotting time.

ENSETE

FOLIAGE HOUSE PLANT
see page 3

leaf up to 1.5 m long

E. ventricosum

Abyssinian Banana

TYPES

Ensete ventricosum leaves have a midrib which is red on the underside. The variety **maurelii** is more popular — leaves have a red tinge.

This banana-like tree is for a large conservatory and not the living room — in a large tub it can reach 2 m when mature. The paddle-shaped leaves can be 60 cm wide, so it is not surprising that this plant needs regular feeding and copious watering during the growing season. Neither flowers nor fruits develop on pot plants.

SECRETS OF SUCCESS

Temperature: Warm or average warmth — at least 12°C in winter.
Light: Bright light — some direct sun.
Water: Water regularly from spring to autumn. Water sparingly in winter.
Air Humidity: Mist leaves frequently.
Repotting: Repot, if necessary, in spring.
Propagation: Not practical.

Ensete ventricosum maurelii

ERIOBOTRYA

FOLIAGE HOUSE PLANT
see page 3

lance-shaped leaf 20 cm long

E. japonica

Loquat

TYPE

Eriobotrya japonica is the only species available. Flowers and fruits will be produced if the conditions are right. It can reach 2 m when mature.

The Loquat tree is grown commercially for its edible oval fruits, but it is grown as a house plant mainly for its decorative leaves — deeply veined and dark green above, and covered with reddish hairs below. The 2 cm wide white flowers appear in winter and are followed by oval yellow fruits. Not easy to find, but it is in the catalogues.

SECRETS OF SUCCESS

Temperature: Average warmth — at least 12°C in winter.
Light: Brightly lit spot or light shade — some direct sun is acceptable.
Water: Water regularly from spring to autumn. Water more sparingly in winter.
Air Humidity: Mist leaves occasionally.
Repotting: Repot, if necessary, in spring.
Propagation: Take stem cuttings in spring.

Eriobotrya japonica

ERYTHRINA

FLOWERING HOUSE PLANT
see page 3

flower 5 cm long

E. crista-galli

Coral Tree

TYPE

The bright red flowers of **Erythrina crista-galli** are borne in clusters in autumn. It can grow to 2 m or more if left unpruned.

A tall and thorny shrub which has unusual flowers. The basic parts of a pea flower are all there, but they are drastically modified. The standard petal is large and flat, the keel is narrow and tubular, and the wings are small. The leaflets of the 3-part leaves are about 8 cm long and their stalks are spiny. Cut back the stems which die down in winter.

SECRETS OF SUCCESS

Temperature: Warm or average warmth — at least 7°C in winter.
Light: Brightly lit spot — some direct sun.
Water: Water regularly from spring to autumn. Do not water in winter.
Air Humidity: Mist leaves occasionally.
Repotting: Repot, if necessary, in spring.
Propagation: Take stem cuttings in summer.

Erythrina crista-galli

EURYOPS

FLOWERING HOUSE PLANT
see page 3

flower
5 cm
across

A grey-leaved compact shrub with masses of long-stalked daisy-like flowers. The special point about this shrub is that it starts to bloom in early summer and carries on right through to winter. It is almost hardy and does not need to be pampered — trim it to shape once flowering has finished. It will reach 1 m high if left unpruned.

E. pectinatus

Euryops

TYPES

Euryops pectinatus is the one to choose — yellow flowers above 6 cm long feathery leaves. **E. acraeus** has smaller (3 cm across) flowers.

SECRETS OF SUCCESS

Temperature: Cool or average warmth — at least 5°C in winter.
Light: Brightly lit spot — not direct sun.
Water: Water regularly from spring to autumn. Water more sparingly in winter.
Air Humidity: Mist leaves occasionally.
Repotting: Repot, if necessary, in spring.
Propagation: Take stem cuttings in spring.

Euryops pectinatus

FEIJOA

FLOWERING HOUSE PLANT
see page 3

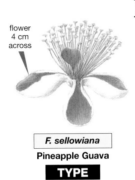

flower
4 cm
across

A shrub grown for its interesting leaves and flowers. The leaves are dark green above and covered with white wool below. The curious flowers appear in late spring. The 4 petals are red on the inside and white on the outside — at the centre of each one is a prominent display of yellow-tipped red anthers. The edible fruits are oval.

F. sellowiana

Pineapple Guava

TYPE

Feijoa sellowiana is the only species sold as a house plant. It will reach 1 m or more if left unpruned. May be listed as **Acca sellowiana**.

SECRETS OF SUCCESS

Temperature: Cool — at least 5°C in winter.
Light: Brightly lit spot or light shade — some direct sun is acceptable.
Water: Water regularly from spring to autumn. Water more sparingly in winter.
Air Humidity: Mist leaves occasionally.
Repotting: Repot, if necessary, in spring.
Propagation: Take stem cuttings in summer.

Feijoa sellowiana

GRISELINIA

FOLIAGE HOUSE PLANT
see page 3

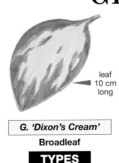

leaf
10 cm
long

There is nothing out of the ordinary about the all-green species, but there are some colourful varieties. You are more likely to find it in the shrub section of your garden centre than among the house plants. The leathery leaves are oval and have a glossy surface. It will grow to 1 m or more if left unpruned — good for a cool, semi-shady spot.

G. 'Dixon's Cream'

Broadleaf

TYPES

The leaves of the basic species **Griselinia littoralis** are all-green. **Variegata** (white/green) and **'Dixon's Cream'** (yellow/green) are available.

SECRETS OF SUCCESS

Temperature: Average warmth or cool — keep cool (at least 3°C) in winter.
Light: Brightly lit spot or semi-shade — avoid direct sun.
Water: Water regularly from spring to autumn. Water more sparingly in winter.
Air Humidity: Mist leaves frequently.
Repotting: Repot every year in spring.
Propagation: Take stem cuttings in summer.

Griselinia littoralis

HARDENBERGIA

FLOWERING HOUSE PLANT
see page 3

This climber has appeared in the garden centre as a house plant, but its need for support makes it more at home in the conservatory. The wiry stems bear 10 cm long lance-shaped leaves and in spring there are masses of small flowers in loose clusters. Cut back after flowering if space is limited — it will reach 2 m high if left unpruned.

pea-like flower 1 cm across

H. violacea

Coral Pea

TYPES

Hardenbergia violacea has pale violet flowers with pale green centres. There are white (**alba**) and pink (**'Pink Cascade'**) varieties.

SECRETS OF SUCCESS

Temperature: Cool or average warmth — at least 5°C in winter.
Light: Brightly lit spot or light shade.
Water: Water regularly from spring to autumn. Water more sparingly in winter.
Air Humidity: Mist leaves occasionally.
Repotting: Repot, if necessary, in spring.
Propagation: Take stem cuttings in summer.

Hardenbergia violacea

HEDYCHIUM

FLOWERING HOUSE PLANT
see page 3

This spectacular plant belongs in the conservatory rather than the living room. In summer and autumn the flower-heads appear on top of the upright stalks, each one bearing scores of 5 cm long red-stamened flowers. The clump grows about 1.5 m high and the leaves are up to 30 cm long. Cut down stems which have borne blooms once flowering is over.

flower-head 30 cm high

H. gardnerianum

Ginger Lily

TYPES

Hedychium gardnerianum is the most popular species. Others include the white-flowering **H. coronarium** which has larger but fewer blooms.

SECRETS OF SUCCESS

Temperature: Cool or average warmth — at least 10°C in winter.
Light: Lightly shaded spot — avoid direct sun.
Water: Keep moist at all times during the growing season, but water more sparingly in winter.
Air Humidity: Mist leaves frequently.
Repotting: Repot, if necessary, in spring.
Propagation: Divide clumps when repotting.

Hedychium gardnerianum

HIBBERTIA

FLOWERING HOUSE PLANT
see page 3

You will find this tall climber in a number of plant catalogues but not at the garden centre — grow it in the conservatory or let it twine around a screen in the home. The solitary flowers appear in summer and occasionally throughout the year. The open seed pods are decorative. Trim back in winter if it is necessary to keep the plant in check.

flower 5 cm across

H. scandens

Guinea Flower

TYPE

Hibbertia scandens is the only species you are likely to find. The shiny dark green leaves have silky hairs below and the flowers are bright yellow.

SECRETS OF SUCCESS

Temperature: Cool or average warmth — at least 10°C in winter.
Light: Brightly lit spot.
Water: Water regularly from spring to autumn. Water more sparingly in winter.
Air Humidity: Mist leaves occasionally.
Repotting: Repot, if necessary, in spring.
Propagation: Take stem cuttings in summer.

Hibbertia scandens

IPOMOEA

FLOWERING HOUSE PLANT see page 3

Ipomoea indica

flower
10 cm
across

I. indica

Dawn Flower

TYPE

The usual house-plant perennial species is **Ipomoea indica** (**I. acuminata**). Purple flowers appear above the heart-shaped 5–15 cm long leaves.

Ipomoea is generally grown as an annual and thrown away after flowering — see The House Plant Expert (page 72). However, there are perennial types which provide a succession of large funnel-shaped flowers from June to October. Perennial Ipomoeas are vigorous climbers and need the support of canes, wires or trellis work.

SECRETS OF SUCCESS

Temperature: Average warmth. Keep cool in winter — at least 7°C.
Light: Brightly lit spot — some direct sun.
Water: Keep moist at all times during the growing season, but water more sparingly in winter.
Air Humidity: Mist leaves occasionally.
Repotting: Repot, if necessary, in spring.
Propagation: Sow seeds in spring.

JOVELLANA

FLOWERING HOUSE PLANT see page 3

Jovellana violacea

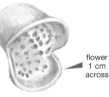

flower
1 cm
across

J. violacea

Jovellana

TYPES

Jovellana violacea is the most popular species. The pale violet flower has a purple-spotted yellow throat. **J. sinclairii** has red-spotted white flowers.

An erect and neat semi-evergreen shrub with attractive flowers in summer. It is sometimes grown against a sunny wall in the milder parts of the country, but it is rarely seen as a conservatory or house plant. The toothed leaves are about 4 cm long and the bell-shaped flowers are borne in terminal clusters. Trim back after flowering to keep in check.

SECRETS OF SUCCESS

Temperature: Cool or average warmth. Keep cool in winter — at least 5°C.
Light: Brightly lit spot or light shade.
Water: Water regularly from spring to autumn. Water more sparingly in winter.
Air Humidity: Mist leaves occasionally.
Repotting: Repot, if necessary, in spring.
Propagation: Take stem cuttings in summer.

LAGENARIA

FLOWERING POT PLANT see page 3

Lagenaria siceraria

bottle-shaped or globular fruit

L. siceraria

Bottle Gourd

TYPES

Lagenaria siceraria (**L. vulgaris**) is the basic species — numerous others can be obtained from specialist seed suppliers.

This is an annual climber to grow in a sunny room or conservatory if you are fond of novelties. The large white petals of the summer flowers only open in the evening. In autumn these flowers are followed by large fruits, and they are the reason why the plant is grown. These bottle gourds or calabashes are used for storing liquids in tropical countries.

SECRETS OF SUCCESS

Temperature: Average warmth or warm — a minimum temperature of 18°C is required.
Light: Choose the sunniest spot available — shade from midday summer sun.
Water: Keep moist at all times.
Air Humidity: Mist leaves frequently.
Repotting: Not required — dispose of plants after fruiting.
Propagation: Sow seeds in spring.

LAMPRANTHUS

FLOWERING HOUSE PLANT *see page 3*

flower 6 cm across

L. spectabilis
Ice Plant

The large daisy-like flowers of this low-growing succulent open only when the sun shines on them. The narrow fleshy leaves are round or triangular in cross-section — they are 3–8 cm long, depending on the species. There is a wide range of flower colours from which to make your choice — the blooms are borne in summer above the foliage.

TYPES

Lampranthus spectabilis (crimson) is the most popular species — there are white and peach-coloured varieties. **L. aureus** has orange flowers.

SECRETS OF SUCCESS

Temperature: Average warmth. Keep cool in winter — at least 5°C.
Light: Choose the sunniest spot available.
Water: Water regularly from spring to autumn — keep almost dry in winter.
Air Humidity: Misting is not necessary.
Repotting: Only repot when essential.
Propagation: Take stem cuttings in spring or summer.

Lampranthus spectabilis

LAPAGERIA

FLOWERING HOUSE PLANT *see page 3*

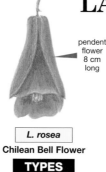

pendent flower 8 cm long

L. rosea
Chilean Bell Flower

The waxy bell-shaped flowers hang from the stems — growing them along horizontal wires in a conservatory is recommended. The twining stems can reach 3 m or more and the flowers appear almost all year round. Direct sunlight should be avoided and it will not thrive in above average temperatures. Use soil-free compost when repotting.

TYPES

Lapageria rosea is the only species available — the petals are rose-pink. There are varieties in other colours, such as **albiflora** and **'Nash Court'**.

SECRETS OF SUCCESS

Temperature: Cool or average warmth — at least 7°C in winter.
Light: Lightly shaded spot.
Water: Keep moist at all times during the growing season, but water more sparingly in winter.
Air Humidity: Mist leaves occasionally.
Repotting: Repot, if necessary, in spring.
Propagation: Sow seeds taken from fruits.

Lapageria rosea

LEPTOSPERMUM

FLOWERING HOUSE PLANT *see page 3*

5-petalled flower 1 cm across

L. scoparium
Tea Tree

You will find this evergreen plant in the shrub section of your garden centre and not with the house plants. In May and June the tiny leaves are covered by masses of small flowers — each one has a central cup with a ring of pink stamens. The blooms may be single or double, and there are many varieties. Prune when flowering is over.

TYPES

Leptospermum scoparium has white flowers. The coloured varieties are more popular — look for **'Kiwi'** (dark red) or **'Jubilee'** (pink).

SECRETS OF SUCCESS

Temperature: Cool — at least 5°C in winter.
Light: Brightly lit spot but shade from hot summer sun.
Water: Water regularly from spring to autumn. Water sparingly in winter.
Air Humidity: Mist leaves occasionally.
Repotting: Repot, in lime-free compost, in spring.
Propagation: Take stem cuttings in summer or sow seeds in spring.

Leptospermum scoparium *'Jubilee'*

LEWISIA

FLOWERING HOUSE PLANT *see page 3*

Lewisia cotyledon

flower 4 cm across

L. cotyledon

Lewisia

TYPES

Lewisia cotyledon is the most popular species. Choose one of the showy hybrids, such as the **'Sunset'** strain. **L. tweedyii** has 6 cm wide apricot blooms.

Lewisia is a rock garden plant which is not easy to keep alive outdoors as it tends to rot in winter. You can enjoy this plant by growing it indoors — the dainty striped flowers are borne on 30 cm high stems in late spring. These stalks arise from a rosette of fleshy leaves. Make sure the crown of the plant is above the compost.

SECRETS OF SUCCESS

Temperature: Cool or average warmth — keep cool in winter.
Light: Brightly lit spot — no direct sun.
Water: Keep moist at all times during the growing season, but water very sparingly in winter.
Air Humidity: Do not mist the leaves.
Repotting: Repot in spring.
Propagation: Sow seeds in spring.

LOTUS

FLOWERING HOUSE PLANT *see page 3*

Lotus berthelotii

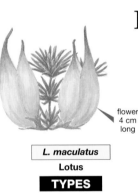

flower 4 cm long

L. maculatus

Lotus

TYPES

Lotus maculatus has orange-tipped yellow flowers — you are more likely to find **L. berthelotii** which has silvery-green leaves and red flowers.

A trailing plant which is an excellent choice for a hanging basket. The leaves are divided into small narrow leaflets and the flowers are eye-catching. There are two species grown as house plants, and both bear blooms which are distinctly claw-like — the flowers appear along the 60 cm long stems in early summer. Lotus is not an easy plant to grow.

SECRETS OF SUCCESS

Temperature: Cool or average warmth — at least 8°C in winter.
Light: Brightly lit spot — some direct sun.
Water: Keep moist during the growing season but water very sparingly in winter.
Air Humidity: Mist leaves occasionally.
Repotting: Repot, if necessary, in spring.
Propagation: Take stem cuttings in spring.

LUCULIA

FLOWERING HOUSE PLANT *see page 3*

Luculia gratissima

L. gratissima

Luculia

TYPES

Luculia gratissima blooms in winter and is more popular than the larger white-flowered species **L. grandiflora** which blooms in summer.

flower 3 cm across

An unusual flowering shrub — you will have to look through the specialist catalogues if you want one for your conservatory. The oval 20 cm long leaves have prominent veins and the flowers are carried in large clusters. They appear at the end of the year and have a pleasant scent. Cut the stems back after flowering has finished to keep the plant in check.

SECRETS OF SUCCESS

Temperature: Cool or average warmth — at least 8°C in winter.
Light: Lightly shaded spot — avoid direct sun.
Water: Water regularly from spring to autumn. Water sparingly in winter.
Air Humidity: Mist leaves occasionally.
Repotting: Repot, if necessary, in spring.
Propagation: Take stem cuttings in summer.

METROSIDEROS

FLOWERING HOUSE PLANT
see page 3

flower 3 cm long

The main recognition feature of this evergreen shrub is the display of prominent stamens on the flowers. The flowers are not large, but when they open in late spring and summer the gold-tipped red anthers provide a colourful powder-puff display. The 5–10 cm long oval leaves are glossy green above and grey below.

M. excelsus

New Zealand Christmas Tree

TYPES

Metrosideros excelsus is not widely available — choose one of the variegated-leaved varieties. **M. robustus thomasii** is similar.

SECRETS OF SUCCESS

Temperature: Cool — at least 5°C in winter.
Light: Brightly lit spot or light shade, but shade from hot summer sun.
Water: Water regularly from spring to autumn. Water more sparingly in winter.
Air Humidity: Mist leaves occasionally.
Repotting: Repot, if necessary, in spring.
Propagation: Take stem cuttings in summer.

Metrosideros excelsus

MUEHLENBECKIA

FOLIAGE HOUSE PLANT
see page 3

leaf 1 cm long

A new house plant for the 21st century which remains a rarity. It is a sprawling plant with wiry stems (hence the common name) and small rounded leaves. These leaves are dark green with brown margins — the tiny flowers are borne in clusters in summer. A plant for hanging baskets or clothing supports for people who like something different.

M. complexa

Wire Vine

TYPES

Muehlenbeckia complexa is the one to grow. **M. plabyclada** is quite different — it has ribbon-like stems and tiny scale-like leaves.

SECRETS OF SUCCESS

Temperature: Cool or average warmth — at least 5°C in winter.
Light: Brightly lit spot or light shade.
Water: Water regularly from spring to autumn. Water more sparingly in winter.
Air Humidity: Mist leaves occasionally.
Repotting: Repot, if necessary, in spring.
Propagation: Take stem cuttings in summer.

Muehlenbeckia complexa

MURRAYA

FLOWERING HOUSE PLANT
see page 3

fruit 1 cm long

Murraya is a familiar indoor bonsai tree (see page 34) but it is also available as a standard house plant for the conservatory or a large room. The leaves are made up of a number of 5 cm long leaflets and the fragrant white flowers are borne in clusters. These bell-shaped 1 cm long blooms are followed by oval red fruits. They are not edible.

M. paniculata

Orange Jasmine

TYPE

Murraya paniculata is the species sold as a house plant for its glossy leaves, flowers and fruit. It can grow to 1 m if left unpruned.

SECRETS OF SUCCESS

Temperature: Warm or average warmth — at least 10°C in winter.
Light: Brightly lit spot — not direct sun.
Water: Water regularly from spring to autumn. Water more sparingly in winter.
Air Humidity: Mist leaves frequently.
Repotting: Repot, if necessary, in spring.
Propagation: Take stem cuttings in summer.

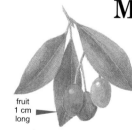

Murraya paniculata

NANDINA

FLOWERING HOUSE PLANT
see page 3

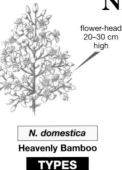

flower-head
20–30 cm
high

Nandina domestica

N. domestica

Heavenly Bamboo

TYPES

Nandina domestica is an upright evergreen shrub with leaves made up of numerous 5 cm long leaflets. Look for the variety **'Fire Power'**.

Nandina is a plant you will have to buy from the shrub section at your garden centre — it will grow in the house or conservatory and provide a changing display throughout the year. The foliage is coppery in spring, green in summer and red in autumn. Clusters of tiny white flowers appear in summer and these are followed by red berries.

SECRETS OF SUCCESS

Temperature: Prefers cool conditions — keep in an unheated room in winter.
Light: Brightly lit spot or light shade — avoid direct sun.
Water: Water regularly from spring to autumn. Water more sparingly in winter.
Air Humidity: Misting is not necessary.
Repotting: Repot in spring.
Propagation: Take stem cuttings in summer.

OLEA

FOLIAGE HOUSE PLANT
see page 3

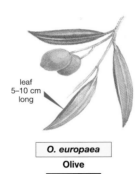

leaf
5–10 cm
long

Olea europaea

O. europaea

Olive

TYPE

Olea europaea is the only species available. It will grow up to 3 m in a large tub, so cut back every spring if it has to be kept in check.

An olive tree makes an interesting feature in a conservatory. It is grown primarily for its grey-green leathery leaves — the small white flowers appear in late summer and they are followed by the well-known oval fruits. It is not difficult to grow if you have space and an unheated well-lit area, but Olea does not flower or fruit on immature specimens.

SECRETS OF SUCCESS

Temperature: Cool — at least 5°C in winter.
Light: Brightly lit spot — some direct sun.
Water: Water regularly from spring to autumn. Water more sparingly in winter.
Air Humidity: Mist leaves occasionally.
Repotting: Repot, if necessary, in spring.
Propagation: Take stem cuttings in summer or sow stones in spring.

PACHIRA

FOLIAGE HOUSE PLANT
see page 3

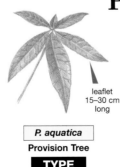

leaflet
15–30 cm
long

Pachira aquatica

P. aquatica

Provision Tree

TYPE

Pachira aquatica is sometimes sold as a cane cutting which forms a crown of leaves after planting — other name: Shaving Brush Tree.

This unusual house plant is grown for the display of large leaves radiating from the top of a thick woody stem. Each leaf consists of 6–9 lance-shaped leaflets arranged like spokes around the long leaf stalk. Pachira requires moist air and regular watering in summer, but even if conditions are ideal it will not produce its spectacular flowers indoors.

SECRETS OF SUCCESS

Temperature: Average warmth. Keep cool in winter — at least 7°C.
Light: Brightly lit spot — not direct sun.
Water: Keep moist at all times during the growing season, but water more sparingly in winter.
Air Humidity: Mist leaves frequently.
Repotting: Repot, if necessary, in spring.
Propagation: Use stem pieces as cane cuttings.

PACHYPODIUM

FOLIAGE HOUSE PLANT
see page 3

Pachypodium lamerei

strap-like
leaf
20–30 cm
long

P. lamerei

Pachypodium

TYPE

Pachypodium lamerei is the easiest species to grow as a house plant. The white flowers appear only on large mature specimens.

An unusual rather than an attractive plant — worth looking for if you collect succulents. The swollen body grows up to 20 cm high and is covered with 3 cm long spines, giving it a cactus-like appearance. At the top of the plant is a leafy crown. Leaves fall when mature and are replaced by new ones. Take care — the sap is poisonous.

SECRETS OF SUCCESS

Temperature: Warm or average warmth — at least 15°C in winter.
Light: Choose the sunniest spot available.
Water: Keep moist during the growing season but water sparingly in winter.
Air Humidity: Do not mist the leaves.
Repotting: Repot, if necessary, in spring.
Propagation: Not practical.

PANDOREA

FLOWERING HOUSE PLANT
see page 3

Pandorea jasminoides

flower
5 cm
across

P. jasminoides

Bower Plant

TYPES

Pandorea jasminoides is the basic species — look for the varieties **alba** (pure white), **rosea** (pink) or **variegata** (cream-marked leaves).

Once this charming evergreen climber was available only from specialist nurseries, but it is now sold by some garden centres. The leaves are made up of 3 cm long leaflets and the flowers are open-faced trumpets — white with a dark pink throat. These blooms appear in small clusters in spring and summer. Avoid drastic pruning.

SECRETS OF SUCCESS

Temperature: Average warmth. Keep cool in winter — at least 12°C.
Light: Brightly lit spot — not direct sun.
Water: Water regularly from spring to autumn. Water more sparingly in winter.
Air Humidity: Mist leaves occasionally.
Repotting: Repot, if necessary, in spring.
Propagation: Take stem cuttings in summer.

POGONATHERUM

FOLIAGE HOUSE PLANT
see page 3

Pogonatherum paniceum

strap-like
leaflet
8 cm
long

P. paniceum

House Bamboo

TYPE

Pogonatherum paniceum is the only species you will find — if the conditions are right flowering spikes may appear.

This grassy plant is available in both Britain and the U.S, but you will have to search for a supplier. It looks like a species of bamboo, but it is much more closely related to sugar cane. The key feature is its long blades of soft green leaflets which arch gracefully downwards. Not showy, but it does provide a delicate background to colourful plants.

SECRETS OF SUCCESS

Temperature: Prefers cool conditions — keep in an unheated room in winter.
Light: Brightly lit spot — not direct sun.
Water: Water regularly from spring to autumn. Water more sparingly in winter.
Air Humidity: Mist leaves occasionally.
Repotting: Repot every year in spring.
Propagation: Divide clumps when repotting.

POLYGALA

FLOWERING HOUSE PLANT *see page 3*

Polygala myrtifolia

flower
3 cm
long

P. myrtifolia

Milkwort

TYPES

Polygala myrtifolia is the only species you will find and the variety **grandiflora** is the type sold as a house plant.

An evergreen shrub which is worth growing — the plant is in flower from May to October and even when not in bloom it is attractive. The odd-shaped flowers are pea-like although Polygala does not belong to this family — the purple and white blooms are borne in small clusters on the stem tips. It will reach about 60–90 cm but it can be pruned in early spring.

SECRETS OF SUCCESS

Temperature: Cool or average warmth — at least 5°C in winter.
Light: Brightly lit spot — some direct sun.
Water: Keep moist at all times during the growing season, but water sparingly in winter.
Air Humidity: Mist leaves occasionally.
Repotting: Repot, if necessary, in spring.
Propagation: Take stem cuttings in summer.

PORTULACA

FLOWERING POT PLANT *see page 3*

Portulaca grandiflora

flower
2 cm
across

P. grandiflora

Sun Plant

TYPE

Portulaca grandiflora is the basic species — buy it as a pot plant from the garden centre in spring or grow it at home from seed.

A colourful annual grown for its summer flowers. The fleshy leaves are about 3 cm long and the blooms are available in a range of colours. Seed is usually bought as a mixture and both single and double forms are usually included. A windowsill is essential — the petals only open when the sun is shining. Portulaca grows about 15 cm high.

SECRETS OF SUCCESS

Temperature: Average warmth.
Light: Choose the sunniest spot available — a south-facing windowsill is ideal.
Water: Water regularly during the growing season but be careful not to overwater.
Air Humidity: Misting is not necessary.
Repotting: Not necessary.
Propagation: Sow seeds in spring.

PROSTANTHERA

FLOWERING HOUSE PLANT *see page 3*

Prostanthera cuneata

flower
2 cm
across

P. cuneata

Mint Bush

TYPES

Prostanthera cuneata (white) is the smallest species. The taller-growing ones such as **P. melissifolia** (mauve) are freer flowering.

This Australian plant is easy to grow and it is listed in numerous catalogues, but it is a rarity at the garden centre. The foliage is aromatic, hence the common name, and the sprays or clusters of cup-shaped flowers appear in spring or summer. The tall varieties of this evergreen shrub are usually trained against a conservatory wall.

SECRETS OF SUCCESS

Temperature: Cool or average warmth — at least 5°C in winter.
Light: Brightly lit spot.
Water: Water regularly from spring to autumn. Water more sparingly in winter.
Air Humidity: Mist leaves occasionally.
Repotting: Repot, if necessary, in spring.
Propagation: Take stem cuttings in summer.

Pseudopanax lessonii
'Gold Splash'

PSEUDOPANAX

FOLIAGE
HOUSE PLANT
see page 3

toothed
leaflet
5–10 cm
long

P. lessonii
Pseudopanax

TYPES

Pseudopanax lessonii is one of several species — the variety **'Gold Splash'** has yellow-veined leaflets. **P. discolor** has bronzy leaves.

Look for it if you are a collector of unusual types. The leaflets radiate from each long leaf stalk like spokes on an umbrella, and there are two reasons for pruning Pseudopanax every spring. It is a tall-growing plant and usually has to be kept in check, and the juvenile leaves are larger than the foliage on old branches. Small flowers and fruits may appear.

SECRETS OF SUCCESS

Temperature: Warm or average warmth — at least 10°C in winter.
Light: Brightly lit spot — some direct sun.
Water: Water regularly from spring to autumn. Water more sparingly in winter.
Air Humidity: Mist leaves occasionally.
Repotting: Repot, if necessary, in spring.
Propagation: Sow seeds in spring.

Pyrostegia venusta

PYROSTEGIA

FLOWERING
HOUSE PLANT
see page 3

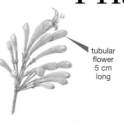

tubular
flower
5 cm
long

P. venusta
Flaming Trumpets

TYPE

Pyrostegia venusta is the only species you will find. The tip of each long flower in the cluster splits into 5 reflexed petals.

A showy climber with clusters of flowers from late autumn to early spring. It climbs by means of tendrils and it does need space. Left unchecked it will grow into the roof of the conservatory or sun room, so it may be necessary to cut back flowering shoots once the display is over. The leaves are made up of 2 or more oval 5 cm long leaflets.

SECRETS OF SUCCESS

Temperature: Warm or average warmth — at least 12°C in winter.
Light: Brightly lit spot — some direct sun.
Water: Water regularly from spring to autumn. Water more sparingly in winter.
Air Humidity: Mist leaves frequently.
Repotting: Repot, if necessary, in spring.
Propagation: Take stem cuttings in summer.

Quisqualis indica

QUISQUALIS

FLOWERING
HOUSE PLANT
see page 3

flower
5 cm
long

Q. indica
Rangoon Creeper

TYPE

There is just one species sold as an indoor plant — **Quisqualis indica**. It will grow to 3 m or more if left unchecked.

This plant is a vigorous climber like Pyrostegia described above, but this one is available at some garden centres. There is a good display of foliage, but Quisqualis is grown for its summer flowers. These narrow tubes open at the tip into 5 petals — they are white on opening day, pink on the next day and on the third day they are rich red.

SECRETS OF SUCCESS

Temperature: Warm or average warmth — at least 12°C in winter.
Light: Brightly lit spot — some direct sun.
Water: Water regularly from spring to autumn. Water more sparingly in winter.
Air Humidity: Mist leaves frequently.
Repotting: Repot, if necessary, in spring.
Propagation: Take stem cuttings in spring.

RHODOCHITON

FLOWERING HOUSE PLANT
see page 3

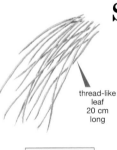

flower
5 cm
long

R. atrosanguineum

Bell Vine

TYPE

The only available species is **Rhodochiton atrosanguineum**. The calyx is a pink cup — the purple petals at the centre form a long tube.

A colourful climber for covering supports or for growing in a hanging basket. The 10 cm long leaves are heart-shaped with leaf stalks which act as tendrils, and the flowers appear in late summer and occasionally at other times of the year. It will grow to about 1.5 m and will attract attention, but it is a short-lived plant. It can be grown as an annual.

SECRETS OF SUCCESS

Temperature: Average warmth — at least 5°C in winter.
Light: Brightly lit spot.
Water: Water regularly from spring to autumn. Water more sparingly in winter.
Air Humidity: Mist leaves frequently.
Repotting: Repot, if necessary, in spring.
Propagation: Take stem cuttings in summer or sow seeds in spring.

Rhodochiton atrosanguineum

SCIRPUS

FOLIAGE HOUSE PLANT
see page 3

thread-like
leaf
20 cm
long

S. cernuus

Weeping Bulrush

TYPE

Scirpus cernuus is grown for its leafy display, although tiny brownish flowers do appear on the thin stems.

The place for this weeping evergreen rush is on a pedestal or in a hanging basket, although you are more likely to find it with a plastic tube at the base to provide a palm-like effect. One of the features of this plant is that you don't have to worry about overwatering — the pot can be kept in a water-filled saucer if the room is reasonably warm.

SECRETS OF SUCCESS

Temperature: Average warmth. Keep cool in winter — at least 7°C.
Light: Brightly lit spot or light shade — provide protection against hot summer sun.
Water: Keep wet at all times.
Air Humidity: Mist leaves frequently.
Repotting: Repot, if necessary, in spring.
Propagation: Divide plant at repotting time.

Scirpus cernuus

SCUTELLARIA

FLOWERING HOUSE PLANT
see page 3

tubular
flower
5 cm
high

S. costaricana

Scutellaria

TYPE

Scutellaria costaricana is the only species which is sold as a house plant — the hardy ones are sold as rockery or border plants.

A colourful flowering plant for a warm room. The dark green 10 cm long leaves are oval and puckered, and the flowers are borne in summer in clusters at the top of the purple stems. Each hooded bloom is red with a yellow throat, and the shrub grows to about 50 cm. Scutellaria becomes leggy with age — cut back bare stems in winter.

SECRETS OF SUCCESS

Temperature: Warm in summer. Keep cooler in winter — at least 15°C.
Light: Brightly lit spot — not direct sun.
Water: Water regularly from spring to autumn. Water more sparingly in winter.
Air Humidity: Mist leaves frequently.
Repotting: Repot, if necessary, in spring.
Propagation: Take stem cuttings in summer.

Scutellaria costaricana

Serissa foetida
variegata

SERISSA

FOLIAGE
HOUSE PLANT
see page 3

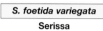

leaf
2 cm
long

A rarity which you will find in a few catalogues — worth searching for only if you want a plant with attractive-looking and evil-smelling leaves. Small, tubular white flowers appear in summer but Serissa is grown for its foliage. The leathery leaves are oval and the bush grows to about 30 cm. Use it as a background plant for showy specimens.

S. foetida variegata

Serissa

TYPES

The only species available is **Serissa foetida** and the variety **variegata** is chosen for its cream-edged leaves.

SECRETS OF SUCCESS

Temperature: Average warmth. Keep cool in winter — at least 7°C.
Light: Brightly lit spot — not direct sun.
Water: Water regularly from spring to autumn. Water more sparingly in winter.
Air Humidity: Misting is not necessary.
Repotting: Repot every year in spring.
Propagation: Take stem cuttings in summer.

Solandra maxima

SOLANDRA

FLOWERING
HOUSE PLANT
see page 3

flower
15–20 cm
long

Grow this climber if you like to have flowers which are really large. It is a vigorous plant which will grow to 3 m or more, and it will be necessary to tie the stems to the support and also to cut back overcrowded stems after flowering. The leaves are 15 cm long and the flowers are spectacular — wide-mouthed yellow trumpets with 5 purple lines inside.

S. maxima

Cup of Gold

TYPES

Solandra maxima is the usual species and is shown here — the flowers of **S. grandiflora** have 10 purple lines within.

SECRETS OF SUCCESS

Temperature: Warm or average warmth — at least 10°C in winter.
Light: Brightly lit spot with some direct sun.
Water: Keep moist at all times during the growing season, but water more sparingly in winter.
Air Humidity: Mist leaves occasionally.
Repotting: Repot, if necessary, in spring.
Propagation: Take stem cuttings in summer.

Sollya heterophylla

SOLLYA

FLOWERING
HOUSE PLANT
see page 3

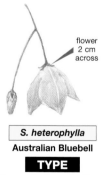

flower
2 cm
across

Many of the climbers described in this book and in The House Plant Expert are giants which are more at home in the conservatory than in the living room, but this is a modest plant which grows to about 1 m. The groups of nodding bell-shaped flowers open in summer — their colour is sky-blue and they are followed by purple fruits.

S. heterophylla

Australian Bluebell

TYPE

Sollya heterophylla is available at some garden centres and can be used to clothe a tall foliage plant.

SECRETS OF SUCCESS

Temperature: Cool or average warmth — at least 8°C in winter.
Light: Brightly lit spot or light shade.
Water: Keep moist at all times during the growing season, but water more sparingly in winter.
Air Humidity: Mist leaves occasionally.
Repotting: Repot, if necessary, in spring.
Propagation: Take stem cuttings in spring.

TECOMARIA

FLOWERING HOUSE PLANT *see page 3*

flower
5 cm
long

A spreading plant which you will need to keep in check by trimming back wayward shoots. The glossy leaflets are about 5 cm long and the 5-petalled tubular flowers appear throughout the growing season from spring to autumn. The usual colour is orange-red, but varieties in other colours are available. It may be listed as Tecoma.

T. capensis

Cape Honeysuckle

TYPES

Tecomaria capensis is noted for the brightness of its flowers. The yellow varieties are **aurea** and **lutea**.

SECRETS OF SUCCESS

Temperature: Warm or average warmth — at least 5°C in winter.
Light: Brightly lit spot — some direct sun.
Water: Water regularly from spring to autumn. Water sparingly in winter.
Air Humidity: Mist leaves occasionally.
Repotting: Repot, if necessary, in spring.
Propagation: Take stem cuttings in summer.

Tecomaria capensis

TIBOUCHINA

FLOWERING HOUSE PLANT *see page 3*

flower
8 cm
across

In a warm greenhouse this showy house plant will bloom nearly all year round — in the living room the flat purple blooms with oddly-curved stamens will be present for months during summer and late autumn. The 10 cm leaves and the stems are velvety and the blooms have a satiny sheen. Cut it back hard in spring to keep it bushy.

T. urvilleana

Glory Bush

TYPE

Tibouchina urvilleana is the only species which you will find at the garden centre — other species are rare.

SECRETS OF SUCCESS

Temperature: Warm or average warmth. Keep cool in winter — at least 12°C.
Light: Brightly lit spot or light shade.
Water: Water regularly from spring to autumn. Water sparingly in winter.
Air Humidity: Mist leaves occasionally.
Repotting: Repot, if necessary, in spring.
Propagation: Take stem cuttings in summer.

Tibouchina urvilleana

TRACHELIUM

FLOWERING POT PLANT *see page 3*

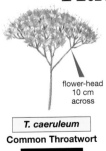

flower-head
10 cm
across

A pot plant to buy in bloom from a garden centre or to raise at home from seed. It can be kept as a perennial, but it is best to treat it as an annual. The plant grows about 40 cm high — in summer large heads of tiny white, mauve or purple flowers are borne on branched stems. Pinch out the tips of young plants to induce bushiness.

T. caeruleum

Common Throatwort

TYPES

The popular variety of **Trachelium caeruleum** is **'Passion in Violet'**. Choose **'Umbrella White'** for white blooms.

SECRETS OF SUCCESS

Temperature: Cool or average warmth.
Light: Brightly lit spot or light shade — provide protection against hot summer sun.
Water: Water regularly during the growing season.
Air Humidity: Mist leaves occasionally.
Repotting: Not necessary. Throw away once flowering is over.
Propagation: Sow seeds in early spring.

Trachelium caeruleum

TRACHELOSPERMUM

FLOWERING
HOUSE PLANT
see page 3

An evergreen twining shrub which is hardy enough to be grown outdoors in mild areas. The white or cream flowers appear above the glossy foliage in summer — the outstanding feature of these star-shaped blooms is their fragrance. The perfume is very strong, but for some people this can result in a headache. It is slow-growing, so don't be impatient.

flower
3 cm
across

T. jasminoides

Star Jasmine

TYPES

The usual species is **Trachelospermum jasminoides**. The flowers are white — for cream-coloured blooms grow **T. asiaticum**.

SECRETS OF SUCCESS

Temperature: Cool or average warmth — at least 5°C in winter.
Light: Brightly lit spot or semi-shade.
Water: Water regularly from spring to autumn. Water more sparingly in winter.
Air Humidity: Mist leaves occasionally.
Repotting: Repot, if necessary, in spring.
Propagation: Take stem cuttings in summer.

Trachelospermum jasminoides

TROPAEOLUM

FLOWERING
HOUSE PLANT
see page 3

The climbing Nasturtium you may find among the house plants at the garden centre is the tuberous one. It will grow to about 2 m or more and has 5 cm wide lobed greyish-green leaves. The spurred flowers on long stalks begin to appear in midsummer. These blooms should be removed when they fade so that the flowering period is extended.

flower
4 cm
long

T. tuberosum

Perennial Nasturtium

TYPE

Tropaeolum tuberosum 'Ken Aslet' is the house plant variety. The yellow petals are brown-veined within and orange-red behind.

SECRETS OF SUCCESS

Temperature: Cool or average warmth — at least 3°C in winter.
Light: Brightly lit spot.
Water: Water regularly from spring to autumn. Water sparingly in winter.
Air Humidity: Mist leaves occasionally.
Repotting: Repot, if necessary, in autumn.
Propagation: Divide tuber when repotting.

Tropaeolum tuberosum

TWEEDIA

FLOWERING
HOUSE PLANT
see page 3

The flowers of this 60 cm high shrub are not large and there is nothing unusual about their shape, but they are still unusual. Tweedia is grown for the changing colour of the flowers as they mature. They begin as pink buds, open to pale blue, become flushed with green and finally change to purple. The heart-shaped leaves are about 10 cm long.

flower
3 cm
across

T. caerulea

Tweedia

TYPE

Tweedia caerulea is not easy to find at the garden centre. It is in some catalogues and can be raised from seed.

SECRETS OF SUCCESS

Temperature: Cool or average warmth — at least 7°C in winter.
Light: Brightly lit spot.
Water: Water regularly from spring to autumn. Water more sparingly in winter.
Air Humidity: Mist leaves occasionally.
Repotting: Repot, if necessary, in spring.
Propagation: Take stem cuttings or sow seeds in spring.

Tweedia caerulea

WATTAKAKA

FLOWERING HOUSE PLANT
see page 3

Wattakaka sinensis

flower
2 cm
across

A fragrant climber for the conservatory with flowers which can be mistaken for Hoya (The House Plant Expert, page 158). The 10 cm wide flower-heads hang down below the grey downy leaves during the summer months. Each white flower has a pink-marked corona at the centre. Unlike Hoya it is frost hardy and may produce pods after flowering.

W. sinensis

Wattakaka

TYPE

You may find **Wattakaka sinensis** at the garden centre. In the plant and seed catalogues it is usually listed as **Dregea sinensis**.

SECRETS OF SUCCESS

Temperature: Cool or average warmth — at least 8°C in winter.
Light: Brightly lit spot or light shade.
Water: Water regularly from spring to autumn. Water more sparingly in winter.
Air Humidity: Mist leaves occasionally.
Repotting: Repot, if necessary, in spring.
Propagation: Take stem cuttings in summer.

WHITFIELDIA

FLOWERING POT PLANT
see page 3

Whitfieldia elongata

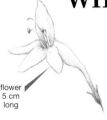

flower
5 cm
long

Whitfieldia is a plant you will find in very few textbooks, but you may find it at your garden centre in spring. It is usually grown as an annual, but you can treat it as a perennial if you have a conservatory where you can maintain warm and moist conditions. The white or red tubular flowers are borne on tall upright stems in summer.

W. elongata

Whitfieldia

TYPE

Whitfieldia elongata (**W. longifolia**) can grow to 2 m or more in a tropical house, but in the home it is a 50 cm high pot plant.

SECRETS OF SUCCESS

Temperature: Warm or average warmth.
Light: Brightly lit spot or light shade — provide protection against hot summer sun.
Water: Water regularly during the growing season.
Air Humidity: Mist leaves (not flowers) frequently.
Repotting: Not necessary. Throw away once flowering is over.
Propagation: Take stem cuttings in summer.

ZAMIOCULCAS

FOLIAGE HOUSE PLANT
see page 3

Zamioculcas zamifolia

leaflet
10 cm
long

You will not find this member of the arum family in the standard house plant textbook, but it is sold by some garden centres. It has become popular with interior decorators as a focal point in a large room — the upright leaves arise directly out of the compost and each one of these leaves bears shiny leaflets arranged in a herringbone fashion.

Z. zamifolia

Zamioculcas

TYPE

Zamioculcas zamifolia is the only species. The stout leaves grow about 60 cm high. Be careful not to overwater.

SECRETS OF SUCCESS

Temperature: Warm or average warmth — at least 15°C in winter.
Light: Light shade.
Water: Allow upper part of compost to dry out between waterings — water sparingly in winter.
Air Humidity: Mist leaves occasionally.
Repotting: Repot, if necessary, in spring.
Propagation: Divide plants at repotting time.

CHAPTER 2
BONSAI

It is hard to resist a mature and well-trained bonsai at the garden centre. A miniature tree with its roots clinging to a rock, or a conifer with gnarled branches on a stout twisted trunk, may seem to be an ideal house plant. The price may put you off, but the thought of root pruning, stem pruning, pinching and wiring should not be a deterrent — these are simple and enjoyable occasional tasks. Nor should you be concerned at the thought of having to keep the pot outdoors for most of the time during the summer and winter months — many varieties can be kept indoors all year round.

There is just one point you should consider carefully before buying. Regular watering is essential, and that can mean every day during summer. Still, you may think that this chore is a small price to pay in order to have such an attractive feature in your home.

CHOOSE THE RIGHT GROUP

Outdoor bonsai

The varieties in this group are not for you if you want plants which you can keep indoors all year round. They are the traditional bonsai with a history dating back a thousand years or more — for many enthusiasts they are the 'real' bonsai.

Outdoor bonsai can be brought indoors for only a few days before they have to be returned to their quarters in the garden. A disadvantage for the house plant lover, but there are a couple of advantages for the bonsai hobbyist. Nearly all the bonsai conifers belong here, and for some styles these tiny-leaved evergreens cannot be rivalled. Secondly, large attractive displays can be created in the garden without the space restriction which applies in the living room.

Indoor bonsai

Pick an example from this group if you want a bonsai which you can keep as a house plant. Nearly all of these plants are trees and shrubs from sub-tropical or tropical areas — they will grow happily under average room conditions although some have their own special requirements which you will find on page 34 or 35. Most can be stood outdoors in a sheltered spot during warm periods in summer.

The usual routine is to buy a trained plant and then to maintain and improve its shape by root pruning, stem pruning, and pinching over the years. Good trees, however, are expensive and it is possible to start from scratch by sowing seeds, using cuttings or converting ordinary nursery stock.

BUYING YOUR BONSAI

Bonsai varieties are not natural dwarfs. They are ordinary trees which will grow to their natural size if they are not properly pruned.

The plant will be expensive. You can raise one from scratch but it will take a number of years. A cheap bonsai will either be young in need of further training or it will be poor quality. It may be ordinary nursery stock which has been cut back, potted and partly trained.

You can go to a traditional plant supplier such as a large garden centre, but seek out a specialist nursery if you plan to become a dedicated bonsai grower.

Make sure you get its name — a label stating 'bonsai' will not do. Find out if it is an indoor or outdoor variety — ask for an information sheet.

Look at the plant — it should be trained in one of the basic styles and the leaves should be green and healthy. Check that the branches are not suffering from die-back. Check that wire is not embedded in the trunk and make sure that the plant is not loose in its pot.

Look at the soil — the surface should be fairly loose, not compacted and waterlogged. The surface should be free of weeds and liverworts.

Look at the pot — the inside should not be glazed and there should be adequate drainage holes in the base.

BONSAI STYLES A–Z

BROOM (Illustrated) Garden tree-like form — regularly branching stems radiate from trunk top

CASCADE (House Plant Expert, page 81) Drooping trunk — reaches below bottom of pot

EXPOSED ROOT (Illustrated) Mature roots visible well above the compost surface in the pot

FORMAL UPRIGHT (House Plant Expert, page 81) Vertical trunk — branches horizontal or drooping

GROUP (Illustrated) A collection of individual trees, each with its own root system

INFORMAL UPRIGHT (House Plant Expert, page 81) Curved vertical trunk — branches on outside of curves

LITERATI (Illustrated) Branches restricted to upper part of attractively shaped trunk

RAFT (Illustrated) A collection of branches rising from a horizontal trunk

ROOT-OVER-ROCK (House Plant Expert, page 81) Rock replaces pot — roots grow into hollows or crevices

SEMI-CASCADE (House Plant Expert, page 81) Drooping trunk — not reaching bottom of pot

SLANTING (House Plant Expert, page 81) Straight or slightly curved trunk sloping to one side

TWIN TRUNK (House Plant Expert, page 81) Two trunks, one smaller than the other, joined at base

TWISTED TRUNK (Illustrated) Trunk distinctly twisted — branches horizontal or drooping

WEEPING (House Plant Expert, page 81) Straight or curved vertical trunk — branches all distinctly drooping

WINDSWEPT (House Plant Expert, page 81) Sloping trunk with all branches on one side

BROOM

GROUP

TWISTED TRUNK

RAFT

LITERATI

EXPOSED ROOT

OUTDOOR BONSAI A–Z

There are hundreds of garden and woodland trees and shrubs which can be trained as bonsai, and there are scores of these varieties which are widely grown in this miniature form. Only a selection of these hardy plants can be included here — the ones listed on these two pages are old favourites which you can either buy or raise from scratch at home.

Varieties of Pine and Maple are the most popular choice, and this underlines the fact that both evergreen and deciduous trees are used. Most of these hardy trees and shrubs are grown for their foliage, and there is a wide range of leaf shapes, textures and colours. There is also no shortage of flowering trees such as Azalea, Wisteria and Crab Apple, and you can also find fruit-bearing types such as Cotoneaster.

ACER

The favourite species is the Japanese Maple (A. palmatum) which is grown for its attractive shape and its lobed leaves which turn red or purple in autumn. The Trident Maple (A. buergerianum) is also widely grown. In summer protect from direct sunlight which would scorch the leaves — in winter protect from strong winds. Prolonged frost should not be a problem. Young branches can be trained by wiring but older ones tend to break. Cut back shoots, as necessary, in summer. Repot and root prune as necessary every 2 – 3 years. Raise new plants from seeds or cuttings.

CHAENOMELES

Japanese Quince (C. speciosa) produces white, pink or red blooms in spring and these may be followed by ball-like fruit — choose a single variety. This familiar deciduous garden shrub is suitable for most bonsai styles and has only one drawback — the sharp thorns make wiring and pruning difficult. Prolonged frost should not be a problem. Wire when required and prune after flowering — do not prune in spring. Repot and root prune as necessary every 2 – 3 years. Raise new plants from seeds or cuttings.

COTONEASTER

The Fishbone Cotoneaster (C. horizontalis) provides year-round interest with its small glossy leaves, pink flowers and then red berries after the leaves turn bronze or red before falling in autumn. Most bonsai styles are suitable — training as a cascade is particularly effective. In winter place in a shed if a heavy frost is expected. Do not overwater, especially in winter. Thin out the branches in summer and wire at any time. Repot and root prune as necessary every 2 years. Raise new plants from softwood or hardwood cuttings.

CRYPTOMERIA

The Japanese Cedar (C. japonica) has horizontal branches and so it is a good subject for an upright style. In summer keep in full sun or partial shade — in winter store in a shed if prolonged heavy frosts are expected. Never let the soil dry out. Cut shoots back in summer to maintain the desired shape. Repot and root prune as necessary every 3 years. Raise new plants from cuttings.

JUNIPERUS

The low-growing Chinese Juniper (J. chinensis sargentii) is the favourite variety of this very popular genus. There are two types of foliage — be careful when handling the sharp-pointed ones. In summer keep in full sun or partial shade. Pinch out buds at the ends of the branches during summer. Repot and root prune as necessary every 3 years. Raise new plants from seeds or cuttings.

LARIX

Larch is not as popular as Pine or Juniper — the probable reason is that it is deciduous. There are advantages — the peeling bark is attractive and the leaves turn yellow before falling. The Japanese Larch (L. kaempferi) is suitable for nearly all styles. Pinch out buds at the ends of the branches during summer. Raise new plants from seeds or cuttings.

MALUS

The Siberian Crab Apple (M. baccata) is an excellent choice if you are looking for a flowering bonsai. The white flowers appear in spring and are followed by small crab apples. In summer keep in full sun or partial shade. Prune new shoots in spring — branches are pruned in autumn. Do not remove fruit spurs. Repot and root prune every 1 – 2 years. Raise new plants from cuttings.

PICEA

Several Spruce varieties can be used, including P. abies and P. jezoensis — all styles except broom are suitable. New shoots should be pinched back in spring and wiring is done in winter. Repot and root prune as necessary every 2 – 3 years. Raise new plants from seeds or cuttings.

PINUS

The Japanese White Pine (P. parviflora) is undoubtedly the queen of the bonsai world — its tiny leaves and purplish bark are to be seen in collections everywhere. New shoots should be pinched back in spring or summer — be careful not to waterlog the soil in winter. Repot and root prune as necessary every 3 – 4 years. Raise new plants from seeds.

PRUNUS

Any of the Japanese Flowering Cherry (P. serrulata) can be grown in miniature form. Wiring is carried out in late spring — branches are shortened as soon as flowering has finished. Pinch out young shoots to maintain shape in summer. Repot and root prune as necessary annually between autumn and spring. Buy new plants or grow from nursery stock.

QUERCUS

Several species are cultivated as bonsai, including the Common Oak (Q. robur). The leaves are large for a miniature tree and they fall in autumn, so bonsai Oaks are not a favourite choice. Wire in winter and pinch back new shoots in summer. Repot and root prune as necessary every 2 – 3 years. Raise new plants from acorns.

RHODODENDRON

The most popular type is the Satsuki or Indian Azalea (R. indica) — a showy display of blooms appears above the glossy evergreen foliage in early summer. Provide protection against strong winds and heavy frost in winter. Prune after flowering. Repot and root prune as necessary every 2 – 3 years. Raise new plants from semi-hardwood cuttings. Grow in lime-free compost.

STEWARTIA

S. pseudocamellia and S. modelpha are both bonsai subjects — they have attractive bark and beautiful autumn leaf colours. The over-large flowers are white. Prune during the dormant season — provide some shade in summer. Repot and root prune as necessary every 2 – 3 years. Raise new plants from seeds or cuttings. Grow in lime-free compost.

ULMUS

Several Elms are grown as bonsai, including U. parvifolia (page 35), U. procera and U. glabra. Nearly all types lose their leaves in winter — prune during the dormant season. Stand in full sun outdoors — U. parvifolia should be protected against heavy frost. Repot and root prune as necessary every 1 – 2 years. Raise new plants from cuttings.

WISTERIA

Both the Chinese Wisteria (W. chinensis) and Japanese Wisteria (W. floribunda) make spectacular bonsai — the drooping clusters of mauve flowers adorn the tree in late spring. You can use either an upright or cascade style. Cut back when flowers fall — repeat pruning of new shoots to maintain shape until the end of summer. Repot as necessary every 2 – 3 years. Raise new plants from cuttings.

ZELKOVA

The Japanese Elm (Z. serrata) is one of the best subjects for the broom style — it is also a good choice for a group bonsai. The bark is grey and the saw-edged leaves are dark green. Keep in full sun or partial shade — protect from strong winds. Cut back branches in winter — trim new growth in summer. Repot and root prune as necessary every 2 – 3 years. Raise new plants from seeds or cuttings.

INDOOR BONSAI A–Z

A number of the bonsai on these two pages are dwarfed versions of well-known house plants which are described in The House Plant Expert. You are much more likely to find them with the African Violets, Ivies and Geraniums rather than on the bonsai table. Examples are Ficus, Bougainvillea, Crassula and Citrus.

The other group are warm climate trees which are usually only available as bonsai — examples include Sageretia, Carmona, Serissa and Murraya. In addition you may find one or two which are frost-hardy — Cupressus macrocarpa 'Goldcrest' and Nandina domestica are to be found with the trees and shrubs as well as with the bonsai at the garden centre.

BOUGAINVILLEA

The Paper Flower (B. glabra) is a tropical climber which is bought as a young plant from the house plant section of the garden centre and then trained by you into one of the bonsai styles. Varieties with red, white and orange blooms are available. Keep cool in winter — a spell outdoors in summer is beneficial. Water regularly, but reduce watering when leafless in winter — tap water is suitable. Root prune every 3 years. Train branches by wiring — cut back over-long shoots in late spring. Raise new plants from cuttings taken in summer.

CARMONA

The Fukien Tea (C. microphylla) is widely available and is renowned for its small and glossy evergreen leaves and attractive shape. The white flowers which appear in late spring are followed by red berries. Winter warmth and a pebble tray are necessary and so is regular watering with rainwater or tap water which has been left to stand — never let the compost dry out. Root prune every 2 years. Carmona has a natural tree-like form with an attractive trunk. Trim back shoots as required — wiring the branches on young plants may be necessary to create a gnarled effect. Raise new plants from seeds or cuttings.

CITRUS

Lemon, Orange or Grapefruit trees can be used. C. mitis is the orange to choose — fragrant white flowers are followed by small orange fruits which are not edible. You are unlikely to find a trained plant — buy the smallest plant you can find in the house plant section and train by pruning and wiring. Standing outdoors in summer is beneficial — keep cool but frost-free in winter. Use rainwater or tepid tap water. Root prune every 3 years. Raise new plants from cuttings. Oranges and lemons can be raised from pips, but flowering will take many years.

CRASSULA

Several Jade Plant species are suitable — C. ovata is widely available as a house plant and the tiny-leaved C. sarcocaulis is a good choice. The flowers are pink or white. Provide as much light as possible and keep cool but frost-free in winter. Misting is not necessary — do not overwater in winter. The plants are shaped by pruning rather than wiring. Crassula does not need the constant year-round care of other types. New plants can be easily raised from cuttings.

CUPRESSUS

Cupressus macrocarpa 'Goldcrest' is unusual — it is a hardy conifer which can be trained as an indoor bonsai. The conical plant has small golden needle-like foliage. You will not find Cupressus with the bonsai plants — buy a small pot-grown one and train it in an upright style. Put in a brightly-lit spot and stand outdoors if possible in summer. Regular misting is essential. Root prune as necessary in spring. Propagation is not practical — buy pot-grown plants.

FICUS

Several species of Ficus can be trained as bonsai — Weeping Fig (F. benjamina) is illustrated. Buy a ready-grown bonsai or get a pot-grown house plant and start from scratch. Wiring will be necessary — large cuts should be treated with a sealant. Trim back new growth regularly to maintain bushiness. Ficus will thrive in a warm room throughout the year — mist the leaves occasionally. Root prune every 2 years. Raise new plants from cuttings in early spring.

MURRAYA

Murraya paniculata (Orange Jasmine) is a flowering evergreen — the leaves are small and the white flowers are fragrant. It is not a difficult plant to care for — any reasonably well-lit spot will do and it does not mind central heating. Repot and root prune as necessary every 2 years. Aim for a tree which is taller than the average bonsai and pinch back regularly to avoid straggly growth. Raise new plants from cuttings.

MYRTUS

Myrtle is one of the easier bonsai to care for — there are small oval leaves, white fragrant flowers and black berries. It will thrive in light shade in the growing season — a cool and bright room is required in winter. Mist the leaves regularly in summer. Use rainwater if the tap water is hard and repot every 2 years using a lime-free compost. Trim back new shoots during the growing season and wire branches on young plants. Raise new plants from seeds or cuttings.

NANDINA

Heavenly Bamboo (N. domestica) is a narrow-leaved evergreen which changes with the seasons — foliage is pink when young, green in summer and purple in autumn. White flowers are followed by red berries. Keep in a well-lit and airy room and mist the leaves regularly in summer. Repot and root prune every 2 years. Prune and pinch back to create an informal upright style. Raise new plants from cuttings.

OLEA

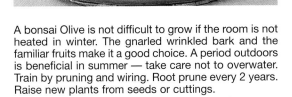

A bonsai Olive is not difficult to grow if the room is not heated in winter. The gnarled wrinkled bark and the familiar fruits make it a good choice. A period outdoors is beneficial in summer — take care not to overwater. Train by pruning and wiring. Root prune every 2 years. Raise new plants from seeds or cuttings.

PINUS

Mediterranean Pine species are occasionally sold as indoor bonsai but they are not suitable for year-round room conditions. Some time must be spent outdoors in summer and an unheated airy spot is needed in winter. The only one you are likely to find is the Aleppo Pine (P. halespensis). Repot and root prune every 2 years. Train by wiring and pruning in any bonsai style. Propagation is not practical — buy pot-grown plants.

PISTACIA

The Mastic Tree (P. lentiscus) is only available in bonsai form — it is a black-fruited evergreen which likes a well-lit unheated room in winter. It does not need to be stood outdoors in summer and is tolerant of both hard water and dry air. Train by pruning and wiring in spring or summer. Root prune as necessary every 2 years. Raise new plants from cuttings.

PUNICA

The Dwarf Pomegranate (P. granatum nana) is a popular bonsai tree with orange tubular flowers and small round fruits. In summer it can be stood outdoors. In winter it needs a resting period when it loses its leaves — keep in a cool room and be careful not to overwater. Train by pruning and wiring in spring. Repot and root prune as necessary every 2 years. Raise new plants from seeds or cuttings.

SAGERETIA

S. thea is a very popular bonsai — it has attractive scaly bark and small evergreen leaves. It thrives in bright light rather than direct sun and can be kept in a heated room in winter. Mist the leaves regularly in summer. You can train the young plant you have bought into any bonsai style by pruning and wiring. Repot and root prune every 2 years. Raise new plants from cuttings.

SERISSA

Tree of a Thousand Stars (S. foetida). This widely available evergreen has box-like leaves and white flowers — quick-growing and easy to train. Provide a well-lit spot away from direct sunlight — some leaf fall may occur if it is moved to a new site. Mist the leaves regularly in summer. Train by pruning and wiring into any style. Repot and root prune every 2 years. Raise new plants from cuttings.

ULMUS

The Chinese Elm (U. parvifolia) is a good choice for the beginner — it will tolerate a wide temperature and light range, and can be trained into any bonsai style. The small evergreen leaves are dark green. Keep it in a brightly-lit spot — it can be stood outdoors in summer. In winter it prefers an unheated room. Train by pruning and wiring. Repot and root prune every 2 or 3 years. Raise new plants from cuttings.

BONSAI AT ITS BEST

Display

With indoor bonsai the general rules of house plant display apply. Place them where their basic light, temperature and humidity needs can be met — see pages 32–35. They are ideally set at close to eye level so that the spaces between the tiers of branches can be clearly seen. Rotate plants occasionally to ensure even growth.

With outdoor bonsai there are several ways to display your trees. The simplest technique is to stand the bonsai pot on the patio or on a coarse sand-covered area in the border. The serious collector, however, requires something more — the usual choice is to stand the pots on slatted staging which is set close to a wall or fence for wind protection. Some form of shading may be erected above, but this must not cut out sunlight for at least part of the day.

Platform-topped posts ('monkey poles') are sometimes used to support individual trees. Eye-catching — but strong winds can topple the pots if they are not secured in some way.

Pots

A bonsai pot has a number of special features. First of all, it is shallow. The exception is the deep cascade pot. Both earthenware and stoneware pots are available — make sure that it is frost-proof if it is to be used for an outdoor variety. Look at the drainage holes — there should be at least twice as much drainage area as you would find at the bottom of an ordinary plant pot. The outside may be glazed or unglazed, but the inside must be unglazed — subdued browns, greens, greys or blues are the experts' choice. Make sure that there are feet at the base of the pot to allow free drainage.

Remember that the appearance of both the tree and the pot are important — read the note on pots above.

Compost

Ordinary garden soil is definitely unsuitable — the easiest plan is to buy a ready-mixed bonsai compost. Ordinary potting compost will not do — the medium for bonsai must be rather coarse and highly absorbent. Enthusiasts generally make their own mixture, often adapting the formula to suit the individual plant's needs. The standard recipe is 50% organic matter and 50% grit. The organic is sifted to give 2 – 4 mm wide particles and may be peat, leaf mould, pine-needle bark or orchid bark. The grit may be washed coarse sand, or flint grit. Some growers add calcined or Akadama clay to the mixture to help water retention.

The tree should look as if it has been taken from a site where it has grown naturally. It may look windswept, the trunk may be contorted, but it should never look obviously pruned and trained.

•

The experts recommend that in a rectangular pot the plant should be closer to one end than the other, but it is a matter of taste. Pot size is important — it must be large enough to look balanced but not so large as to overwhelm the bonsai. Bear in mind that ease of cultivation increases with size of container. Objects (Chinese figures, etc) are a matter of personal taste.

•

Anything which makes the tree look old is desirable. Exposed roots have this effect and sharis and jins (page 38) can add to the feeling of maturity.

•

In an upright style the groups of branches are generally horizontal or drooping to give a cloud effect. There should be air spaces between the 'clouds'.

CARING FOR YOUR BONSAI

Temperature

The temperature requirement of an indoor bonsai is given in the A–Z section on pages 34–35 or in The House Plant Expert A–Z guide of its grown-up sister. The average plant requires the warmth of a standard living room in summer and the cooler conditions you would find in an unheated room in winter. Nearly all bonsai can be stood outdoors in summer — see the note on light. Outdoor bonsai are hardy, but some require protection in a period of heavy frost.

Light

Most indoor bonsai require a brightly lit spot but only some flourish in direct sunlight. All should be protected from hot summer sun. As a general rule a spell outdoors is beneficial in summer, but there should be a transition period — move the pots out for just a short time at first and extend this outdoor period until the plants can be left out for their summer break. For both outdoor and indoor bonsai there should be some shade from the hot midday sun.

Food

The general rules for feeding pot plants in The House Plant Expert apply to bonsai, although the need for regular feeding is generally greater — the pot is unusually small and the compost contains virtually no nutrients. As a general rule use a well-balanced fertilizer in the active growing season but change to a low-nitrogen one in autumn. Feed sparingly in winter. A modern development is the slow-release pellet which removes the need for frequent feeding.

Water

Water when the surface dries out — scratch the compost if you are not sure. Expect to water frequently, perhaps every day, if the container is small, the leaf area is large, the air is warm or the plant has not been repotted for some time. Use rainwater if you can on lime-hating plants. A watering can fitted with a fine rose is the recommended method, although some growers occasionally immerse the pot in a bowl of water for a brief time. Whichever method you use, take care not to keep the compost constantly saturated. With outdoor bonsai you may still have to water after rain if there is a dense canopy of leaves. Watering regularly does not remove the need to maintain a moist atmosphere around the leaves. Frequent misting of the leaves of indoor bonsai is helpful — the most effective method is to stand the pots on a pebble tray (see The House Plant Expert, page 19).

Root pruning & Repotting

The purpose of root pruning is to ensure that the growth above ground and the root system below ground remain in balance. The purpose of repotting is to provide a fresh supply of compost. As a general rule new plants are root pruned yearly and mature plants are treated every 2 – 5 years — see the A–Z section (pages 32–35). The best time is in spring when the buds are beginning to swell — deal with evergreens in March. The exceptions are spring-flowering trees — root prune when flowering has finished.

Remove the tree and gently remove some of the old compost and comb out the outer roots — the traditional tool is a chopstick. About half the compost should be removed. Cut back the roots — about $\frac{1}{3}$ of the root system should be removed.

Thoroughly wash and dry the pot or use a slightly larger one. Cover the drainage holes with fine mesh from your bonsai supplier. Push two wires or pieces of string through the holes and secure on the mesh pieces.

Cover the base of the pot with a thin layer of grit or calcined clay — your pot should now look like the illustration. Put the plant in position and secure it by twisting the wires over the trunk base. Now add fairly dry compost and work it in between and above the roots with your fingers — do not leave any air pockets. Water in gently but thoroughly — keep out of sunlight and do not feed for a month or two.

Wiring

The basics of wiring are simple. Wire is wrapped around a branch which is then bent to the desired position. After a period of time the wire is removed and the branch retains its new shape. In practice it is not so simple — it takes a lot of experience to become an expert. Before tackling your bonsai try your hand on a twig in the garden. Use anodised aluminium wire — start with the thickest branches first. Choose wire which is about one quarter the width of the branch and cut a piece about 1½ times its length. Turn the wire anti-clockwise to grip but not bite into the wood. Bend the wired wood slowly and gently. The right time to remove the wire depends on several factors. As a rough guide wait 1 year for a conifer and about 3 months for a deciduous tree — always remove the wire before it cuts deeply into the wood. Use pincers and remove it piece by piece — do not try to unwind.

Pruning

Maintenance pruning is carried out on an established bonsai in late winter or early spring. Its purpose is to maintain the basic shape and avoid congestion. The first task is to remove some of the outer twigs to leave room for next year's growth, and to remove or shorten branches which are crossing over others and spoiling the shape. Branches which have started to grow upwards can soon spoil the cloud effect of a conifer bonsai and so need to be removed. Be careful with conifers. A cut shoot which is leafless will not produce new growth. Every few years it will be necessary to remove a few of the larger branches to allow twigs to develop. Make sure your tools are sharp. Use scissors or shears for twigs — larger branches will require secateurs or pincer-like branch cutters. Large cuts should be covered with a cut paste.

Branch pruning is usually carried out in autumn and involves the removal of an unwanted branch. Use secateurs, a small saw or a branch cutter to cut off most of the branch to leave a small stub. Remove the stub with a branch cutter to leave a shallow hole — fill this depression with a cut paste.

Generative pruning is carried out on deciduous trees (not conifers) in midsummer. Its purpose is to stimulate the production of new branches. Cut off the trunk or a thick branch at the desired length — in a short time a number of shoots will develop around the cut area. These should be thinned to the desired number in autumn.

Pinching

This technique is carried out during the summer months to maintain the shape of an established tree and to reduce the size of the leaves. Shoot tips are nipped out with your fingernails although you might need a small pair of scissors. The standard routine with deciduous trees is to remove the leaf bud on the shoot tips at regular intervals — with flowering trees it is important not to remove the flower buds.

Sharis & Jins

As illustrated a shari is a dead area of the trunk which has lost its bark. This decorative effect makes the bonsai look older than it really is, and is created by peeling away a strip of bark near the base of the tree — make sure that it is above ground level and does not circle the tree. Seal the edges of the cut area with a cut paste sealant. A jin is a dead branch from which the bark has been stripped.

CHAPTER 3

BROMELIADS

It seems hard to believe that one of the most colourful and exotic house plant families should also be one of the easiest to look after. In fact the first group described below is an answer to the lazy home gardener's prayer — stand them on a pebble tray and they never have to be watered!

On page 40 you will find the second group of Bromeliads — the showy rosette-forming varieties which include all the popular Bromeliad types. On page 42 there is the final group — a small collection of difficult-to-grow earth-hugging varieties which are noted for their colourful foliage.

Three groups, and despite the wide range of sizes and colours they do have one important feature in common. In their natural habitat most of them grow attached to trees and not in the soil, and this means that overwatering and poorly-drained compost are their greatest dangers.

Nearly all are undemanding plants, but it takes patience to persuade a Bromeliad to flower again. Still, it is worth trying — see page 104.

THE AIR PLANTS

Tillandsia caput-medusae

At your garden centre you will see these small grey-leaved plants attached to shells, coral, driftwood etc. The long and narrow leaves are covered with furry scales, and it is these tiny plates which absorb moisture from the air and nutrients from the dust which settles on the foliage. No need for compost and no need for water, but the Air Plants do benefit from regular misting in summer.

All the plants are species of Tillandsia. Keep them in bright light away from direct sunlight and provide a winter temperature of at least 10°C. Once they reach maturity the bright flowering spikes appear and the surrounding leaves may change colour, but the blooms last for only a few days. T. bulbosa and T. tenuifolia have a bulb-like base and produce blue flowers in red bracts. Another type with a bulb-like base is T. caput-medusae which is chosen for its thick, twisted leaves. If you want silvery foliage there is T. ionantha or T. argentea. For long rush-like leaves you should look for T. juncea.

These grey Tillandsias have showy-flowered green-leaved relatives which need watering in the usual way — see page 58.

THE FLOWERING ROSETTES

In a contest to find the ideal house plant you would find this group of the bromeliads in the short list for the top award. The popular ones have large and dramatic flower-heads borne on stalks — this floral display lasts for months and when it is gone there are attractive and often coloured leaves. These varieties are generally undemanding plants which require neither misting nor repotting. They will tolerate some neglect and thrive within a wide temperature range.

A word about the flowers. The true flowers are usually insignificant — the display comes from the bracts, which are flower-like leaves. Once the flower-head fades the rosette from which it arose stops growing and one or more of the offsets at the base starts to develop and will eventually produce a new plant.

AECHMEA

Aechmea chantinii

The Aechmeas and Vrieseas are the favourite bromeliads and the most popular species of all is the Urn Plant (A. fasciata). It has all the properties you would expect — stiff, strap-like leaves and a flower-head which can last from midsummer until early autumn. The grey-green, spiny-edged leaves are banded with silver and the dark pink flower-head with its small purple flowers arises from the vase-like centre of the leafy rosette.

There are other Aechmeas with a variety of leaf and flower colours. A. chantinii has white-banded green leaves and yellow-tipped flowers which last for weeks rather than months. If you want red berries as well as flowers there are A. 'Foster's Favorite' (blue/ orange flowers and purple-red leaves) and A. fulgens discolor (purple flowers and purple-backed leaves). The brown-banded, yellow-leaved A. orlandiana needs winter warmth.

VRIESEA

Vriesea 'Christiane'

Like Aechmea the Vrieseas are popular house plants with attractive strap-like leaves and showy long-lasting flower-heads on upright stalks. The basic species is the Flaming Sword (V. splendens) with a bright red, flattened flower-head and brown-banded 30 cm long leaves. The hybrids are more colourful than the parent and sometimes are multicoloured (yellow/red) and multiheaded — look for V. 'Fire', V. 'Tiffany' and V. 'Charlotte'. V. hieroglyphica is grown for its large green leaves bearing broken brown bands and lines. There is also the diminutive Lobster Claws (V. carinata) with fan-like yellow and red flowers.

Aechmea fasciata

BILLBERGIA

Billbergia nutans

Billbergia has an upright rosette of leaves rather than a wide-spreading one like most other bromeliads. Queen's Tears (B. nutans) is the only one you are likely to find — the 30 cm long grassy leaves are nothing special, but the flowers are. In spring 10 cm long flower-heads in a mixture of green, yellow, purple and pink hang down from 45 cm long stalks. A tough plant which will not suffer in a room at 5°C. The common name comes from the nectar which drops when the flowers are shaken.

GUZMANIA

Guzmania lingulata minor

The glossy arching leaves form a typical bromeliad rosette with a central vase. The stout stalk bears petal-like bracts at the top and a cluster of small white flowers. The Scarlet Star (G. lingulata) is the best known species and a number of varieties are available — 'Cardinalis' (red), 'Splendens' (ivory) etc. The red-flowered ones may have a red-leaved stalk. G. lingulata minor is an attractive red-flowered dwarf. The hybrids are perhaps the best choices for the living room — examples are G. 'Glory of Ghent' and G. 'Orangeade'.

NEOREGELIA

Neoregelia carolinae tricolor

Small flowers cluster in the centre of the leafy rosette of this small and round flower-head giving the name Bird's Nest Bromeliad to this genus and the closely-related Nidularium. During flowering the leaves surrounding the flowers turn red and the colour lasts for months. The usual one is the Blushing Bromeliad (N. carolinae tricolor) — the saw-edged leaves are about 30 cm long. With N. concentrica the central area turns pale purple rather than red. The Fingernail Plant (N. spectabilis) does not follow the usual pattern — the leaves do not change colour at flowering time but the tips are bright pink.

NIDULARIUM

Nidularium innocentii lineatum

Similar to and easily confused with Neoregelia — it differs by having a central rosette of short leaves and only these colour at flowering time to form a distinct flower-head. N. innocentii is the only one you are likely to see, and even this one is hard to find. It is a pity it is not more popular — it is colourful with purple-backed leaves and a bright red flower-head, and it thrives in shade. Not all species have red flowers — N. billbergioides has green-tipped yellow bracts.

THE EARTH STARS

Cryptanthus bromelioides tricolor

The Earth Stars differ in a number of ways from the popular bromeliads described on pages 40 and 41. First of all, their home in the wild is the forest floor and not attached to trees, and their pointed and wrinkled leaves form a flat rosette which hugs the ground. They have none of the adaptability and hardiness of the usual bromeliad — they need warm conditions and compost which is kept constantly moist during the growing season. Most of them like bright conditions but a few relish a shady spot.

All the Earth Stars belong to the genus Cryptanthus. The dwarf C. bivittatus with 10 cm long green-striped leaves is the most popular one — there are also the zebra-striped C. zonatus and the multi-coloured C. bromelioides tricolor. With misting and care they can be grown in pots, but they are more usually found in bottle gardens.

RAISING YOUR OWN BROMELIADS

Raising bromeliads from seed is a truly lengthy business, and it is easier and quicker to produce new plants from offsets, but even here you must be prepared for a long wait before you will have mature plants in flower.

Once flowering is over the plant slowly starts to die and offsets ('pups') are produced at the base — there may be just one, as in the case of Vrieseas, or a cluster. These offsets may be tightly wedged in the axils of lower leaves or they may be at the end of creeping stems — the way they arise does not affect the next step.

When the offset has reached a height of between a quarter and a half of the mother plant, remove it by pulling it away. This may be easier said than done — in some species the offsets come off very easily, but with others it may be necessary to let some of the leaves of the mother plant die down before attempting removal.

The time for this task is during the growing season, although it can be done in winter if the room is heated. Plant the offset in a pot containing a mixture of 1 part moss peat / 1 part coarse sand. Water in and keep it close to the mother plant as it requires the same growing conditions. Repeat watering when the surface begins to dry out — in this case you must water the compost and not the vase at the centre of the leafy rosette.

It is hard to predict how long you will have to wait for the new plant to produce its first floral display. Aechmea fasciata offsets may bloom in the following season, but others may take 5 years or more.

It isn't essential to remove the offsets to ensure a future display from a plant which has finished flowering. The foliage of the rosette slowly dies down but the rootstock remains alive. Remove the old foliage and the offsets will develop into new plants which will eventually produce flower-heads. See page 104 for details.

LOOKING AFTER YOUR BROMELIADS

It is not surprising that in a large family like the bromeliads you will find a few difficult members — some species of Cryptanthus are only happy in the moisture-laden atmosphere of a bottle garden. But the favourite showy varieties are surprisingly easy to look after and can be expected to thrive in ordinary room conditions. This does not mean that each one does not have its own individual likes and dislikes — these are explained below for the popular members of this fascinating family.

Large pots are not necessary and repotting is seldom, if ever, needed. An effective way to display your bromeliads is to create a bromeliad tree on which the plants are wired to the branches — see page 85 in The House Plant Expert for details.

LIGHT

All the bromeliads will survive in partly shady conditions, but each type has its own individual needs if it is to look its best. The Air Plants are at the top of the light scale. They need really bright light — a sunny windowsill is ideal. Next come the varieties with stiff leaves which are banded or variegated — Aechmea fasciata is the best-known example. These plants need good light but not strong sunlight — in shade the attractive markings may be lost. Billbergia is another bromeliad which welcomes a brightly-lit site. The soft-leaved bromeliads such as Vriesea splendens, Guzmania and Neoregelia appreciate light shade — direct sunshine can result in the leaf tips being scorched. Plants such as Aechmea 'Foster's Favorite' with soft and coloured leaves are at the bottom of the light scale — bright light can bleach them.

COMPOST

An open compost which will ensure free drainage and good aeration is vital. Bromeliad enthusiasts make up their own mixture — one part peat and one part coarse sand with perhaps some leaf mould is a widely-used example. If you plan to use a proprietary compost then choose a soilless one and mix in some coarse sand.

TEMPERATURE

The bromeliads are tolerant of warm conditions in summer and nearly all are quite happy if the room is not heated in winter. With stiff-leaved varieties such as Aechmea fasciata there is no problem when the temperature falls as low as 7°C. Neoregelia and Billbergia can be included here, but the softer-leaved types such as Guzmania and the Vrieseas prefer to be kept at 10°C or above. The Earth Stars are the most delicate members of the group and need a minimum of 15°C in winter.

WATER

Everyone agrees that the bromeliads cannot tolerate compost which is kept permanently moist and may appreciate quite dry conditions in winter. But not everyone agrees on the best way to water. The simple routine is to fill the central vase with water, allowing a little of the water to spill over the compost to keep the roots properly anchored. Empty and refill the vase every 1 – 2 months. This routine, however, is frowned upon by some experts, especially if the plant is in flower or if the temperature is very low. They feel that the bromeliads should be watered in the normal way for house plants, allowing the surface to dry out between waterings. Mist the foliage during the summer months.

FEEDING

Feed with a pot plant fertilizer in the normal way, especially at flowering time. The dilute feed can be watered on to the compost or poured into the vase. The natural home for most bromeliads is on the side of trees and not the soil, and so they obtain nutrients through their leaves. You can look after your bromeliads in a similar way by using a dilute fertilizer solution when misting the plants — follow the maker's instructions.

CHAPTER 4

HERBS

Growing herbs in the kitchen is a good if underused idea. You will be able to pick your favourite seasonings and garnishes without having to trudge out to the vegetable plot in winter. If you don't have a garden then for the first time you will be able to cross these herbs off your shopping lists, but best of all you will have the satisfaction of having grown your own.

All very desirable, but these plants should be regarded as productive items like the plants on the allotment rather than decorative items like the house plants in the living room. Most are rather plain, and regular cutting will not enhance their appearance.

The illustrated example has used margarine pots with drainage holes cut in the base to underline the practical rather than the display nature of herbs in the kitchen. You can, of course, use more attractive containers but most herbs are not things of beauty.

DOS & DON'TS

Do give them the growing conditions they need. Nearly all flourish in bright light — a sunny windowsill is ideal. Some but not all require compost which is kept moist at all times — check requirements on page 45.

•

Don't expect them to be permanent residents. The usual life-span is a season, after which they are planted outdoors or thrown away.

•

Do grow in individual pots — herbs with similar growing needs can be grouped together in a container to create a herb garden. Put a layer of grit at the bottom and surround the pots with peat, ground bark or similar material.

•

Do turn the pots once a week to prevent one-sided growth.

•

Don't grow herbs or saladings which you use in large amounts. There is no point in turning your kitchen into a mini-allotment.

Do trim regularly whether you plan to use then or not.

•

Don't remove more than half the foliage at one time.

•

Do buy pots from your supermarket or garden centre — it is so much easier and quicker than sowing seed.

HERBS A–Z

BASIL

An annual herb with a clove-like flavour which is a basic ingredient for many Italian dishes — it can also be used in soups and salads. Use sparingly. Stand the pot on a sunny windowsill and keep the compost moist at all times. Basil needs a warm room — pinch out flowers when they appear.

BAY

Bay is one of the components of bouquet garni and is also used in fish dishes and stews — the tough leaves are removed before serving. Stand the pot on a sunny windowsill and water when the surface of the compost is dry. Water sparingly in winter. Buy a pot-grown specimen and keep in check by regularly pinching out the branch tips. You can as an alternative grow it as a ball- or pyramid-shaped tree to add a decorative touch to one of your rooms. A word of warning — be careful not to buy a laurel as they have poisonous leaves.

CHIVES

The mild-tasting stems of this member of the onion family are used to add flavour and colour to many dishes — potato salad, soups, omelettes, salads etc. Stand the pot on a sunny windowsill and water when the surface of the compost is dry. Water sparingly in winter. When required cut some of the stems to about 2 – 3 cm from the base. Remove flower-heads as they appear.

MARJORAM

The main use for pot marjoram is as a chopped herb for sprinkling on meat or poultry before roasting. It is an easy-to-grow perennial which grows rapidly and needs to be trimmed regularly. Stand the pot on a sunny windowsill and keep the soil moist at all times during the growing season — water sparingly in winter.

MINT

One of our favourite herbs — a popular partner for lamb and garden peas. Stand the pot on a sunny windowsill and keep the soil moist at all times during the growing season — it can be stood in a saucer of water during the summer. Water sparingly in winter. Trim back regularly.

OREGANO

A peppery-leaved perennial herb which is an ingredient of bouquet garni. Stand the pot in a bright spot away from direct sunlight and water when the surface of the compost is dry. Water sparingly in winter.

PARSLEY

Our favourite garnish which has many uses as a flavouring in the kitchen. Seed takes a long time to germinate and so a pot-grown plant or a clump dug up from the garden is the usual starting point. Stand the pot in a bright or lightly-shaded spot away from direct sunlight. Keep the soil moist at all times during the growing season — water sparingly in winter. Treat as an annual — replace each year.

ROSEMARY

A blue-flowered evergreen shrub which is used to flavour lamb, pork and veal. Stand the pot in a bright spot away from direct sunlight and water when the surface of the compost is dry. Water sparingly in winter. The low-growing form Rosmarinus officinalis prostratus is attractive — so is a ball-headed standard tree form in the corner of the kitchen.

SAGE

Sage is used for flavouring meat or as a stuffing ingredient. Pinch out the tips regularly to maintain the bushy growth habit. Stand the pot in a bright spot away from direct sunlight and water when the surface of the compost is dry. Water sparingly in winter.

THYME

This tiny-leaved evergreen has many uses in the kitchen. Stand the pot in a bright spot away from direct sunlight and water when the surface of the compost is dry. Water sparingly in winter.

CHAPTER 5

CHRISTMAS FLOWERS

The sales of flowering pot plants soar as Christmas approaches. Nearly everybody accepts that the old favourites will not become permanent residents, but we feel we must keep them flourishing for as long as possible. This does not always happen. If the conditions are wrong our purchase or present may droop or lose its leaves in just a few days. But even when it has performed well, the usual procedure is to throw the pot away once the display is over. It may be possible to keep them to provide a display next year, but this may not be easy to do and should be undertaken only if you like a challenge.

THE IDEAL CHRISTMAS HOME ...
but they all want something different!

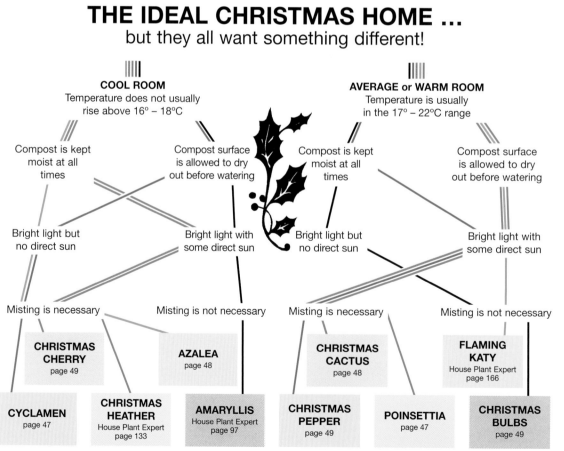

COOL ROOM
Temperature does not usually rise above 16° – 18°C

AVERAGE or WARM ROOM
Temperature is usually in the 17° – 22°C range

Compost is kept moist at all times

Compost surface is allowed to dry out before watering

Compost is kept moist at all times

Compost surface is allowed to dry out before watering

Bright light but no direct sun

Bright light with some direct sun

Bright light but no direct sun

Bright light with some direct sun

Misting is necessary

Misting is not necessary

Misting is necessary

Misting is not necessary

CHRISTMAS CHERRY
page 49

AZALEA
page 48

CHRISTMAS CACTUS
page 48

FLAMING KATY
House Plant Expert
page 166

CYCLAMEN
page 47

CHRISTMAS HEATHER
House Plant Expert
page 133

AMARYLLIS
House Plant Expert
page 97

CHRISTMAS PEPPER
page 49

POINSETTIA
page 47

CHRISTMAS BULBS
page 49

CYCLAMEN

The swept-back petals of Cyclamen flowers have a special charm. White, pink or pale red and frequently stained with a deeper hue, they rise on long stalks above the marbled leaves. Varieties with frilly-edged flowers are available, and so are fragrant dwarfs which grow to no more than 10 – 15 cm.

A lovely plant for Christmas, but take care. Flowers soon droop and leaves turn yellow in a centrally-heated room. As a general rule, if you are really comfortable then the Cyclamen on the table is not! The ideal temperature is 13° – 16°C with a minimum of 5°C. If the temperature is going to rise above 16°C you must keep the air moist — stand the pot on a pebble tray or surround the pot with damp peat in an outer container.

Coupled with cool conditions it needs bright light away from direct sunshine — a north-facing windowsill is ideal. Faulty watering stands alongside air which is too warm as the main cause of drooping stems and an early end to flowering. Watering by immersion is the best method (page 113), but you can water from above if you take care to avoid soaking the top of the tuber. Use soft water if you can and repeat watering when the surface has dried out.

When the flowering season is over there is no need to throw the plant away. The tuber can be rested and brought back into growth for next Christmas — see page 105.

POINSETTIA

Poinsettia has become the house plant symbol of Christmas. You will find them in millions of homes — usually red but white, cream and pink varieties are sold and so are compact dwarfs.

The showy coloured bracts which surround the small true flowers should remain for at least a couple of months, but so often the leaves droop and the bracts drop at the beginning of the New Year. This may not be your fault — plants will fail if they have been stood outdoors or have become chilled on the way home from the store.

In most cases the cause of failure is faulty conditions and/or treatment. Poinsettias need to be kept warm — 13° – 22°C is ideal. They also need moist air, so mist the leaves frequently. Double potting is a good idea — place the pot in a large container and surround with damp peat. Good light is essential — some direct sunshine is acceptable.

The trick in getting a Poinsettia to last for months is to learn how to water it properly. Let the upper half of the compost become dry before watering thoroughly. Not a dribble — let the water drain away and then water it again. Finally, there are two pet hates to avoid — cold draughts are harmful and so is the hot and dry air close to a radiator.

Once flowering is over the plant is discarded. It is possible to keep a Poinsettia from one year to the next but this is a complex process involving controlling the day-length. See The House Plant Expert (page 195) for details.

AZALEA

Azaleas are one of a trio of Christmas favourites — like Cyclamen they require cool conditions to ensure a long floral display, and they share with Poinsettias the need for an out-of-the-ordinary watering routine. The two techniques, however, are poles apart — Poinsettias need to be almost begging for water before the watering can comes out, whereas the compost housing Azaleas must be kept really moist at all times. This means that they require watering about two or three times a week, or even daily if the pot is small and the room is rather warmer than recommended. Water by the immersion method if the compost has started to dry out. Use rainwater or water which has been boiled and left to cool.

The ideal temperature range is 6° – 16ºC — somewhat higher temperatures can be tolerated if you water as described above and keep the leaves misted daily with tepid water. Stand your pot in a well-lit spot away from direct sunlight, and remove flowers by twisting off (not cutting) when they fade.

Many varieties of Azalea (Rhododendron simsii) are available. Don't buy a plant which is in full flower — look for one with many more buds than open flowers and you will be able to enjoy the display for a month or even more. But the time will come when the blooms are gone, and this is one of the Christmas plants you should not throw away. You can harden it off and plant in the garden or you can keep it as a pot plant to bloom again next year — see page 104.

CHRISTMAS CACTUS

The Christmas Cactus looks nothing like its spiny relatives — it has a drooping growth habit and the flattened stems look like leaves. Its natural home is the forest and not the desert, and that explains the difference in appearance and cultural requirements.

There has been some confusion over the years about the naming of this winter-flowering cactus — the best plan is to regard them all as hybrids of Schlumbergera. The flowers are about 3 cm long — red or pink with swept-back petals. The blooming period is between November and late winter — the Easter Cactus is in flower during April and May.

Christmas Cactus is an easy plant to care for without any fussy demands when in flower. Average room temperatures are fine with an ideal range of 12° – 22ºC in any brightly-lit spot — some direct sunshine is acceptable. Water thoroughly when the compost begins to dry out, but do not keep it constantly soaked. An easy plant to care for, but there are things to avoid. Hot and dry air can cause the buds and flowers to drop, so mist the leaves regularly if the room is warm. Moving the plant from place to place can have a similar effect — leave it alone once it has started to flower.

Many of the plants bought for Christmas are thrown away once the flowering season is over and the rest are kept in the hope that they will bloom again next year. This is possible, but not if you treat them like any other house plant. The proper routine is fairly complex — see page 104 for details.

CHRISTMAS CHERRY & CHRISTMAS PEPPER

Two plants which are similar in a number of ways, but they are not related. Christmas Cherry (Solanum capsicastrum or S. pseudocapsicum) belongs to the potato family and Christmas Pepper (Capsicum annuum) is a member of the pepper family.

These compact bushy plants bear fruits that have developed from small white flowers which appeared in spring. The round fruits of Christmas Cherry are orange-red when mature (warning — they are poisonous) and the oval or pointed fruits of Christmas Pepper may be yellow, orange, red or purple (warning — they are not poisonous, but they are hot).

Both need to be kept moist at all times and misting the leaves frequently will help to extend the display period — both dry soil and dry air can cause the fruits to drop. Bright light with some direct sunshine is another cultural requirement they share, but their temperature requirements differ. Christmas Cherry likes cool conditions, ideally 10º – 15ºC. Capsicum prefers warmer conditions — 15º – 22ºC is its preferred range.

By following the rules your colourful display should last for two or three months, but by late winter or early spring the fruits will be gone. The next step with Christmas Pepper is quite simple — just throw them away. Christmas Cherry plants are also usually thrown away, but you can keep them for fruiting again next year — see page 105 for details.

CHRISTMAS BULBS

There is something special about having a bowl of bulbs in full flower on Christmas Day. The usual way to do this is to plant specially-prepared bulbs, but there is a small group which are naturally early-flowering and can be expected to bloom before the end of the year. These are the Tazetta group of Narcissi which bear several small flowers on each stem.

For a much wider range you must buy bulbs which have been specially prepared for Christmas flowering — Hyacinths, Narcissi and Tulips are available. Plant them no later than the end of September and follow the standard forcing technique. The bowls must be kept cool and dark — you can put them in a black plastic bag in a shed. Check occasionally to see that the compost is still moist and to see if shoots have appeared. When they are about 3 cm high move the bowls into a cool room — this should be before December. Transfer to their chosen home when the flower buds have formed. The ideal spot is bright without direct sunshine in a room which is not too warm. Aim to keep the compost moist but not wet. Turn the bowls occasionally to avoid lop-sided growth. Once flowering is finished the bulbs are usually thrown away — this is the right thing to do with Hyacinths. You can keep Narcissi and Tulips for planting in the garden next year. To do this, feed the plants with a rose or tomato fertilizer until the leaves have died down and then remove, dry and store the bulbs until the autumn for planting outdoors.

CHAPTER 6

ORCHIDS

Orchids were once just for the rich and knowledgeable, but not any more. Once they were found only in greenhouses and conservatories, but not any more — orchids are now one of the top three in the list of our favourite house plants. There are several reasons for this dramatic increase in the popularity of these exotic plants. First of all, there is now a large selection of varieties for growing in the home and some of the newer hybrids are much more tolerant of ordinary room conditions than the traditional ones. Next, these orchids are now widely available — you will find them in garden centres, supermarkets, florists, DIY superstores and on market stalls everywhere. Finally there has been the realisation that the blooms can last for months and even a modest collection can provide flowers all year round. You can grow Cymbidium for autumn to spring flowers, Paphiopedilum for spring to autumn flowers and Phalaenopsis for flowers at various times during the year.

The word 'orchid' usually conjures up a picture of a large and beautiful flower in tropical surroundings, but the range of orchid types, habitats and so on is vast. They grow from the arctic to the equator, and range in size from rambling giants to ground-hugging dwarfs. Most are epiphytes, growing on the bark of trees — the rest are terrestrials, growing in the soil or on leaf litter. The one thing they have in common is their basic flower anatomy — one lipped petal which is often ornate, plus two other petals and three sepals which may or may not be similar to each other in size and colour.

There are two approaches to orchid growing. You can treat them as long-lasting pot plants to be disposed of after flowering, and that makes care a simple matter. Or you can aim to keep them as permanent house plants which will bloom year after year — this calls for more attention to air humidity, feeding, repotting etc. Work to do, then, but the results are so rewarding.

CARING FOR YOUR ORCHIDS

Each orchid has its own cultural requirements — Paphiopedilum is easy to care for but the beautiful Cattleya is a challenge. There are some general requirements, and these are shown below. Resting is an additional need if you want your plants to bloom again — see page 106. There are four general hates — draughts, strong summer sun, poor drainage and direct radiator heat.

Temperature

There are cool-growing types which require a minimum temperature of 10°C and at the other end of the scale the tropical-growing ones need a minimum of 17°C. As a general rule your orchids will thrive at a temperature where you are comfortable — ideally there should be a 10° – 15°C difference between the day and night temperature. Most types benefit from a spell outdoors between June and September in a sheltered spot out of the sun.

Light

From spring to autumn the general requirement is a brightly lit spot away from direct sunlight. There are exceptions — plants from the forest floor such as the Jewel Orchid will thrive in quite shady conditions whereas Cymbidium needs summer sun when not in flower. In winter it will be necessary to move the plant closer to the window as some direct sun is no longer a problem. Always grow orchids in a room which is lit at night during winter.

Water

You can water either by the immersion method (see page 113) or in the traditional way with a watering can. It is essential to allow the plant to drain fully before putting it back on its saucer or in its holder — root rot resulting from standing water is one of the main causes of orchid death. Aim to keep the compost moist at all times, although the surface may be dry. Water about once a week — more in summer, less in winter. Use tepid soft water.

Air Humidity

Orchids need a moist atmosphere and that can be a problem in a centrally-heated room. With an 'easy' type such as Paphiopedilum you can get away with misting the leaves frequently in summer and occasionally in winter, or by surrounding the pot with other house plants. For more demanding orchids, however, a pebble tray is necessary, as shown in the illustration on page 79 and described in The House Plant Expert (page 19). Sponging the leaves occasionally with tepid water will provide additional help, but for some tropical varieties the only satisfactory answer is to grow them in a glass-sided container known as a terrarium — see page 92.

Food

Orchid compost does not contain fertilizer. Avoid the temptation to overfeed — as a general rule feed with an orchid fertilizer or half-strength pot plant fertilizer with every third watering — decrease in spring and autumn and stop in winter. Do not feed a newly-potted plant for at least a month.

Dead-heading

With most orchids you should cut off flowering stems near the base once the blooms have faded. With Phalaenopsis the stem should be cut a little below the bottom flower so that it will be able to flower again on the same stalk.

Repotting

Don't be in a rush to repot — this should take place about every 2 years when the pseudobulbs have reached the rim of the container. Spring is the recommended time. The new pot should not be much larger than the old one and you will need to buy a special orchid compost. This will be a bark mix, a rockwool mix or sphagnum peat plus perlite. Gently pull the plant out of its pot (as illustrated) and cut away any damaged roots. Pot up in the usual way (see The House Plant Expert, page 13), taking care not to press the compost down too tightly. Lightly water from the top to settle the orchid into the new pot before returning it to its home. Use tepid water.

PROPAGATION

Symbodial Orchids

Most orchids belong here. At the base there is a creeping rhizome which joins together the pseudobulbs. These are swollen stem bases from which the leaves and the flower stalks arise. New pseudobulbs appear as growth progresses — old pseudobulbs turn brown after flowering has finished and these backbulbs remain for several years. You can divide the plant at repotting time — each clump should contain at least 3 leafy pseudobulbs and these should be potted up in the usual way (see page 51). Staking may be necessary. Think before deciding to divide your orchid instead of repotting. Division will give you more plants, but you will miss at least one flowering season.

Monopodial Orchids

A few types do not produce pseudobulbs. Flowers and leaves appear on a single stem, and as this stem grows it may produce a succession of blooms for many years. Cut off the leafy top of the stem in spring and use as a cutting if the plant has grown too tall — the cut stem of the mother plant will in time form a new head with leaves and flowers. This, of course, means a loss of flowering seasons, and so it is preferable to look for rooted offsets at the base and use as planting material.

Slab Display

On page 39 and in The House Plant Expert (page 85) a bromeliad tree is illustrated and described. This method of growing these bark-clinging plants is a novel way of allowing them to live as they do in their natural home. Orchids can be treated in the same way, but watering poses a problem. With a bromeliad the vase in the middle of the rosette can be kept filled with water, but orchids do not have this growth pattern. It is therefore more usual to use a slab of wood or bark as the base — the watering procedure is to immerse the slab in a bucket of tepid water for about 10 minutes once a week and then allow to drain before replacing it on the wall.

The starting point is a piece of wood, tree branch or piece of bark — attach a suitable metal hanger at the back. Divide the orchid (see Propagation on this page) and wrap the roots of a clump with moist sphagnum moss — tightly attach the moss-covered roots to the slab with plastic-covered wire. Keep in a shady spot for a week or two and then move it to its permanent home.

BRASSIA

It is not difficult to see why B. verrucosa is called the Spider Orchid. The thread-like petals and sepals give it a most unusual appearance for an orchid, and yet it is one of the easiest to grow. The 10 cm wide pale green flowers are borne on graceful sprays — the aroma is either sweet or unpleasant, depending on personal taste. Flowering begins in late spring, and there should be a period of rest when the blooming period is over — give less water until growth restarts. It will thrive at ordinary room temperatures and it can be kept cool in winter — minimum 10°C. Place the pot in a bright spot away from direct sunlight. A number of hybrids of Brassia are available.

CAMBRIA

You will find the name Cambria on the label of long-stemmed plants which are available wherever orchids are sold, but you will not find it in most books. It is a plant which does not occur in nature — it is a hybrid of other orchid genera and is more correctly known as Vuylstekeara. The long-lasting flowers are available in various shapes and sizes — the flower stalks require support. A windowsill is a favourite site for this plant — provide shade against direct sunlight in summer. Cambria should be kept in a room which is lit after dark in winter. The minimum winter temperature is 13°C. The compost must never be allowed to dry out — reduce but do not stop watering in winter.

CATTLEYA

The white Cattleya bloom is the Corsage Orchid — the largest of all orchid flowers in cultivation. Waxy and with a frilled and colourful lip it is the showpiece of the orchid world, but not all Cattleyas are giants. There are miniature ones and there is a wide range of colours — always choose a hybrid as they are much easier to grow than the species. Flowering times range from spring to autumn, depending on the variety — the flowers last for about 3 weeks. Let it rest after flowering for about 6 weeks by giving less water. The minimum winter temperature should be 13°C — place the pot in a bright spot with morning or evening sun. Wipe the leaves occasionally with tepid water.

CYMBIDIUM

The original hybrids were large ungainly plants — these have now been replaced by the mini varieties as house plants which are available in a wide range of colours. Mini-Cymbidiums are recommended for beginners as they will withstand more neglect than other types. There are 20 or more blooms on each upright stem and the flowers last for 8–12 weeks. The flowering period is autumn and winter — let it rest after flowering by giving less water. Put the plant outside in a semi-shady spot in summer, and in winter keep it in a cool room with a minimum temperature of 10°C. Cymbidium needs a bright spot with some morning or evening sun.

DENDROBIUM

The genus Dendrobium is an author's nightmare. There is a multitude of species with a variety of heights, flower shapes and colours, and flowering times which range from early spring to late winter. Some can thrive in a winter temperature as low as 10ºC whereas others need 16ºC or more. Finally, your plant is probably evergreen but it may lose its leaves after flowering. As a general rule keep the plant in a bright spot away from direct sunlight and let it rest after flowering, but the best advice is to make sure you buy a named variety with instructions. The most popular ones are the D. nobile varieties with white or pink flowers in spring. Keep cool and dry in winter.

LYCASTE

L. aromatica can be used to add variety to your orchid collection. The all-yellow flowers are borne singly on 20 cm high stems, and they are noted for their strong scent. The plant grows actively in summer and needs both warmth and ample water. It must be kept cool and very little water is needed in winter when the flowers appear and the leaves fall. Mist the leaves regularly when the plant is growing and keep it in an area where there is light shade. The largest flowers (15 cm across) are borne by L. virginalis which is the easiest species to grow — this plant should be kept completely dry in winter. In addition to the species there are many large-flowered hybrids in a range of colours.

MILTONIA

Miltonia species are difficult to care for and are best left to the commercial grower or orchid enthusiast with a greenhouse. They do not like temperature fluctuations and demand constantly moist air. Fortunately there are Miltonia hybrids nowadays and these are much less demanding — stand the pot in a bright spot away from direct sunlight and ensure a minimum temperature of 13ºC in winter. The fragrant blooms measure 4–8 cm across and have a pansy-like appearance — hence the common name Pansy Orchid. The usual colours are white, pink and red and the usual flowering time is May-July. The arching stems may need some support.

ODONTOGLOSSUM

Many of the species, such as O. crispum and O. cervantesii, have beautiful flowers but are not easy to grow. The problem is that their native home is in the mountains and not in the jungle, and so they need cool conditions in order to thrive — they suffer when the temperature exceeds 20º – 22ºC. The hybrids are less demanding and can be grown in the living room. Put the pot in a bright spot away from direct sunlight and increase the interval between watering when they are not in flower. Aim for a winter temperature of at least 13ºC. Odontoglossum varieties are not as popular as many of the plants described here — some (the Tiger Orchids) have striped petals.

ONCIDIUM

Some of the Oncidium species are quite spectacular with their butterfly-like flowers — O. papilio and O. tigrinum are examples. The problem is that they are difficult to grow and are best avoided for growing in the home. The hybrids, however, will succeed in a bright but sunless location if you provide good ventilation and some means of increasing the humidity around the plants during the growing season. Allow the plant to rest after flowering by reducing watering and keeping the pot in a cool room. Aim for a minimum winter temperature of 10°C. The tall spikes of the hybrid varieties bear numerous flowers which are usually quite small.

PAPHIOPEDILUM

The well-known Slipper Orchid with its pouched flowers differs from other popular house plant types in two ways. There are no pseudobulbs, so it must be kept reasonably moist throughout the year. It is also the only common terrestrial orchid (see page 50) and so is not suitable for slab display (see page 52). Each flower stalk bears a single 5–10 cm wide bloom which lasts for 8–12 weeks — there are many hybrids from which to make your choice. If you have a warm, centrally-heated room pick one with mottled leaves — all-green varieties are for cool locations. A minimum winter temperature of 13°C is required. A brightly lit spot away from direct sun is necessary.

PHALAENOPSIS

You will find Phalaenopsis everywhere that orchids are sold. The flat-faced flowers are borne on arching stems, each bloom lasting for about a month. The hybrids on offer are easy to grow, and with proper care will flower intermittently all year round. Popularly known as the Moth Orchid, it needs a bright but sunless spot with a minimum winter temperature of 18°C — Phalaenopsis does not enjoy the cool nights favoured by some other types. It will grow quite happily with day temperatures as high as 28°C, but give it a rest period by putting it in a room with a lower temperature than its usual home for a few weeks in autumn. Do not cut off the roots growing outside the pot.

ZYGOPETALUM

Zygopetalum is not one of the popular group of orchids so don't expect to find it at your local garden centre or DIY superstore. It is, however, worth looking for if you are building up a varied collection as it has a heavy fragrance and the flower lip has unusual violet-coloured stripes. The petals and sepals are green with large brown blotches. They are generally large plants with flower spikes reaching a height of 45–60 cm. The flowers usually appear in winter and last for about a month. Do not mist the leaves — use some other method for creating high humidity around the plant. For guidance on temperature, water and light requirements see the rules for Cymbidium on page 53.

CHAPTER 7

SPECTACULAR FLOWERS

For many people one of the attractions of growing vegetables in the garden is the challenge of trying to produce roots, pods, heads etc which are bigger, longer or heavier than normal. Even in the flower garden it is a point of pride to have the largest dahlias, the biggest roses or the earliest daffodils in the neighbourhood.

None of these goals has a place in the mind of the average house plant grower. Abnormal size is not generally the aim — the quest here is to persuade the plants to repeat the floral display after the blooms have faded and it has had time to rest. Still, there are times and occasions when we do want a flower or a floral display to be 'spectacular' — that is, capable of making the visitor stop and stare. A combination of large size and bright colour is the usual feature which makes a plant spectacular, but a novel shape without unusual size or colour can be equally capable of grabbing attention. Examples of both types of spectacular flowers are illustrated on the following pages — grow them by all means, but do remember that good condition coupled with freedom from pests and diseases is more important than with plants which people are not expected to notice.

THE BIG & BEAUTIFUL

Here you will find the large blooms that cannot fail to be noticed. In some cases they are single true flowers — Datura and Amaryllis are examples. Some others have a flower-head made up of many small flowers — Jacobinia and Haemanthus belong here. Finally there is the coloured bract group such as the Bromeliads — the display here is due almost entirely to showy flower-like leaves with small true flowers between or above them. One important group of showy plants is not included — these are the free-blooming types which owe their colourful appearance to the sheer mass of blooms. Popular ones include Azalea, Pot Chrysanthemum, Cineraria, Bougainvillea and Jasmine.

THE ODD & UNUSUAL

The dividing line which separates these eye-catching house plants from the big and beautiful ones is not a clear cut one. The Bird of Paradise (Strelitzia) and the Passion Flower (Passiflora) both have flowers which have an unusual shape and are therefore included here, but these blooms are also large and colourful — they really belong in both camps. A number of plants have unusual blooms which are attractive but are certainly not large — the group with flowers like powder-puffs is an example. Finally there are the oddities which would never win a prize in a beauty contest — the Insect Catchers and Bat Plant are included. These are classed as spectacular flowers solely because of their bizarre appearance.

THE BIG & BEAUTIFUL

Orchids

All orchid flowers are beautiful, but not all are big. Turn to a Cattleya, Cymbidium or Paphiopedilum hybrid (illustrated) if you want large blooms, but there are also varieties with flowers measuring 3 cm or less. Few plants are more spectacular than orchids — see Chapter 6.

Calla Lily

The upturned trumpets of the Calla or Arum Lily are 15–20 cm long, standing above the large arrow-shaped leaves. The white species Zantedeschia aethiopica was once a popular choice but it does not like central heating — choose instead one of the coloured hybrids. Despite its exotic appearance it is an easy plant to grow. Stop watering in winter and keep the pot as warm as possible. Repot in spring — the tubers can be divided at this stage to provide extra plants.

Haemanthus

Perhaps the Blood Lily (H. katharinae) is the biggest ball flower of all. The 20 cm wide flower-head is made up of scores of small starry blooms with prominent stamens. Plant the bulb with the nose just above the surface and water liberally during the growing season. Remove the stalks when the summer flowers have faded and keep watering until the leaves turn yellow. Water very sparingly and stand the pot in a cool place during this resting period.

Datura

The giant hanging bells which grace this woody plant in summer are truly impressive. Each fragrant flower is 20–30 cm long and they are available in yellow and pink as well as the more usual white. Both single- and double-flowered varieties are available. This is a plant for the conservatory and not the living room, as it needs lots of space. Grow it in a large tub and cut it back hard in winter — take care, all parts including the sap and seeds are poisonous. The usual choice is D. candida (Angel's Trumpet) or D. suaveolens — both may be listed as Brugmansia.

Hibiscus

The key recognition feature is the long central column bearing the anthers. The usual width is about 10 cm and a wide range of colours and forms are available. Choose H. rosa-sinensis cooperi if you want variegated leaves, but the pick of the bunch is H. schizopetalus with pendent blooms bearing fringed red petals. With good light, feeding, watering to keep the compost moist and occasional misting you can expect a blooming period from May to October. Cut back in winter and keep cool and fairly dry at this time to ensure an abundant floral display next year.

Medinilla

Spectacular is the only word to describe the pink flower-heads of Medinilla magnifica which hang from the stems in late spring. The small flowers are borne below and between the papery bracts — a floral display reaching a length of 45 cm or more. It does need space and it is fussy about winter warmth — not less than 15°C but not much more than 20°C. Let it rest during this winter period by watering sparingly.

Amaryllis

The Amaryllis which is sold as a large bulb for potting is really a Hippeastrum hybrid. The 15–20 cm wide trumpets open on tall stout stalks before the leaves — keep the pot in a cool place to prolong the life of the blooms. The plants are usually thrown away after the winter or spring flowers have faded, but they can be kept to provide flowers next year. Continue to water and feed in a sunny spot, but in winter stop watering and put in a cool and shady place.

Bromeliads

The bromeliads share with orchids the distinction of being the top group for big and beautiful flowers. The flower form, however, could not be more different — a showy collection of colourful bracts instead of a single bloom. The range of bold bromeliads grown as house plants is illustrated in Chapter 3. An additional type which belongs here are the large relatives of the lowly Air Plants. Tillandsia lindenii (illustrated) has flattened pink flower-heads which are about 25 cm long. T. cyanea is smaller.

Hymenocallis

There is no mistaking this plant — the 10 cm wide central cup looks like a white Narcissus but the outer petals are thin and curled, giving rise to its common name — Spider Lily. Pot up the bulbs in winter with the tips level with the compost surface. The blooms appear on tall stalks between April and June — after flowering the frequency of watering should be reduced. A winter rest period is needed. With types which keep their leaves it will be necessary to water sparingly, and with the varieties which die down keep the compost dry until the start of the year.

Caesalpinia

This S. American plant shares its common name (Bird of Paradise) with Strelitzia, but its flower form is very different. The tall flower-heads bear numerous yellow-petalled flowers which are crowned with prominent bright red stamens. Despite its hot-house appearance it will thrive in average or cool conditions and is easy to grow. You can raise it from seed if you cannot find a plant at the garden centre.

Canna

These showy pot plants are usually regarded as exotics for the garden rather than as plants for the home, but it has few rivals as an eye-catching specimen in the conservatory. The decorative paddle-shaped leaves add to the display provided by the large flowers in yellow, orange, pink or red. Plant the tubers in late winter and keep the plants regularly watered and fed during the growing season. Stop watering when the foliage dies down in the autumn and store the plants in their pots over winter.

Dipladenia

It may say Dipladenia on the label, but the plant you have bought is really a species or variety of Mandevilla. For the largest flowers choose M. splendens or one of its hybrids — the white or pink trumpet-shaped blooms are about 10 cm wide. Keep the plant well-lit, watered and fed for a summer-long display — keep it in a reasonably cool spot in winter and cut back the long stems if you want to maintain a bushy habit.

Hedychium

The Ginger Lilies are a flamboyant genus with a variety of flower shapes. The usual one is H. gardnerianum which has the largest flower spike (30 cm or more) but not the largest flowers. These are yellow with prominent red stamens — the butterfly-shaped white blooms of H. coronarium are larger but there are only about five on each flower spike. Cut down the stems after flowering and let the plant rest over winter — water very sparingly. Repot every other spring — the rhizome can be divided at this stage to provide additional plants.

Jacobinia

In late summer the pink plumed heads on top of the leafy stalks of J. carnea (King's Crown) are an impressive sight. The tubular flowers last for several weeks — make sure that the soil is kept moist and the leaves are misted regularly. The stems should be pruned back quite hard once the flowering season is over. In winter water sparingly and in spring it is a good idea to occasionally raise new plants from cuttings as old plants tend to be unattractive.

Epiphyllum

The Orchid Cacti are a good choice only if you are prepared to put up with their untidy growth habit. The flowers do make up for it — multi-tiered open trumpets in a wide variety of colours. These trumpets can be quite short or up to 30 cm long — many are fragrant and some open only at night. Early summer is the usual flowering period and with the proper routine you can get your plant to bloom year after year — see The House Plant Expert for details.

Crinum

A large plant for the conservatory which bears its head-turning flowers in late summer — the blooms last for about a month. The usual species is C. powellii which has 15 cm wide pink trumpets on the top of 1 m high flower stalks. Buy the variety album if you want white blooms. Pot up the bulbs in March with the tip just above the surface. Water liberally during the growing season. In winter move the pot to an unheated room and water very sparingly — repot every 3–4 years.

Anthurium

You can easily recognise this flower from its palette-like shape and central tail. The waxy surface is glossy and the long-stalked blooms have a dramatic effect. They are not easy to grow as they need warm conditions and a moist atmosphere, but are certainly worth the effort. For the largest flowers choose A. andreanum — they may be white, pink or red and the tail is straight or arched. The red-flowered A. scherzerianum with its curly orange tail is easier to grow in an average room, but the blooms are only half the size.

Gloriosa

The Glory Lily is a splendid sight when in full flower in summer. The species to choose is G. rothschildiana. Each 10 cm wide bloom has swept-back petals and a prominent display of sepals — these red petals have yellow wavy edges. Gloriosa is a big plant so you will need a conservatory or large room — you will also have to provide some means of support for the weak stems. After flowering give less water and then stop to let the tuber dry out. Keep at a minimum of 12°C — repot in spring.

Tibouchina

This flower has increased in popularity in recent years, which is not surprising when you look at its large silky blooms which grace the plant from spring right through to autumn. When in flower it really does deserve its common name — Glory Bush. Train it against some form of support or trim it back every year to keep it as a bush. Tibouchina is not difficult to grow — in the growing season give it plenty of water and put it in a slightly shady spot.

Solandra

S. maxima is the species you are most likely to find — it has started to appear at garden centres. The buttercup-yellow open cups are about 15 cm across and there are dark lines within. Its favourite home is the border soil in a conservatory, but it should succeed in a large pot in the house. Put it in a sunny spot and give plenty of water in summer when it is in flower. It may lose its leaves in winter — keep almost dry if it does.

THE ODD & UNUSUAL

Powder-puffs

Several house plants have flower-heads made up of blooms composed of stamens. This gives a powder-puff effect when globular and a bottle-brush effect when the flower-head is elongated. Calliandra inaequilatera (red) is a good example of a powder-puff species — others include Mimosa pudica (pink) and Metrosideros excelsus (red). The Bottle-brush Plant (illustrated) is Callistemon citrinus (red or pink).

Strelitzia

Unmistakable, and the unchallenged queen of the house plant world. The 15 cm orange and purple flowers of S. reginae (Bird of Paradise) look rather like the head of a bird — these blooms open in spring or summer and should last for several weeks. The best plan is to buy a plant in flower — if you start from scratch it may take about 5 years before you see any blooms. Feed and water freely in summer — water sparingly in winter.

Bat Plant

The common name of Tacca chantrieri is Bat Plant because of its curiously-shaped brown bracts and flowers, but its alternative name of Cat's Whiskers is perhaps more appropriate as the flowers have numerous long and pendent threads. Once you could only find Tacca in specialist collections but it is now offered as a house plant. It is not easy to grow — it needs warm and humid conditions, and the soil should be kept moist with tepid soft water.

Stapelia

A plant to look for if you feel you must grow the largest house plant flower available. A potted-up specimen will be hard to find, but there are several seed suppliers. The one to choose is S. gigantea — the star-shaped flower coloured red and yellow measures 25–35 cm across. S. variegata (illustrated) with brown-spotted yellow leaves is a much smaller (8 cm wide) species. Stapelia is distinctly unusual — an additional novelty is the short-lived unpleasant odour of some types, hence the common name Carrion Flower.

Insect Catchers

Several species which are able to catch and extract nutrients from insects are available as house plants. None is easy to grow nor are they particularly attractive, but all are interesting as oddities. The Fly Traps, Sticky-leaved Plants and Pitcher Plants are described in The House Plant Expert (page 162) — the most interesting ones are the Pitcher Plants such as Nepenthes (illustrated). The water-filled flower-like funnel is really a modified leaf. Constantly moist compost, moist air and occasional insects or scraps of meat are the basic requirements.

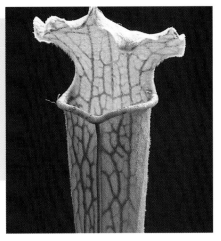

Anigozanthos

This floral curiosity has become available as a house plant in recent years — each woolly segment of the flower bears some similarity to the paw of an animal. Kangaroo Paw is the common name and the various species are recognised by their colour — A. flavidus is yellowish-green often flushed with pink, A. manglesii is bright green with a red base and A. pulcherrimus is yellow with red whisker-like threads. A. rufus (illustrated) has red flowers.

Passiflora

Big and beautiful, but the Passion Flower is distinctly unusual. The arrangement of the flower parts is both colourful and uniquely complex. All summer long the 10-petalled blooms appear on the stems which grow and spread quickly — some form of support and annual spring pruning are essential. Several species are available, including the hot-house P. quadrangularis (Granadilla), but only one (P. caerulea) is a popular house plant. White and purple varieties are available.

Clianthus

The common names of C. puniceus (Parrot Bill and Lobster Claw) refer to the beak- or claw-like shape of the red flowers which open in late spring — see illustration. The variety albus has white blooms. It is an easy plant to grow but it does have a straggly growth habit and needs support. The Glory Pea (C. formosum) also has red claw-like flowers, but the similarity stops there. It is a 60 cm high bush which is difficult to grow as a perennial under standard room conditions.

CHAPTER 8

ROOMSCAPING

Roomscaping. It is doubtful whether you will have heard of the word, which is not surprising as it is not to be found in books and articles on house plants.

What is surprising is the absence of information on the principles of roomscaping, as its brother and sister are known to everyone, and thousands of books have been written about them.

Roomscaping's brother is garden landscaping — the set of rules and recommendations which are used for creating attractive and stylish features in the garden. Landscaping is not about the placing of individual plants — it is about the way they can be grown individually or planted in groups with non-living items to produce attractive features. Some examples of these features are the rockery, herbaceous border, lawn and vegetable plot.

Roomscaping's sister is flower arranging, with millions of people around the world following the rules and recommendations established over the years for creating pleasing features in bowls, vases etc.

To summarise, with garden plants and with cut flowers we set out to create *features* by putting the living items together in ways which the experts tell us is good design. With house plants, however, the idea of creating features rather than finding a suitable home for our plants is hardly touched on in the articles we read, and the rules and recommendations for good design have not been set out in clear terms. Very simply, roomscaping involves understanding and then putting to work the various interior designer rules and ideas which go into the creation of a house plant feature.

At this point there may be a howl of protest. The word 'roomscaping' may not be known but there are lots of articles in magazines and chapters in house plant books on decorating with house plants. This is true, but these dwell on how to position plants effectively for their own well-being and for maximum visual impact. You can easily find lists of suitable plants for the bathroom, kitchen, hall etc, but there is hardly anything on how to use these plants to make a discrete feature. For example, there are scores of books which will tell you which plants to put on a windowsill, but you would have to search hard to find the expert way to create a designer windowsill using house plants. Another example. Interest in outdoor water features has greatly increased during the past decade and it has become a favourite subject for some writers, but an indoor water feature incorporating house plants is hardly ever seen or mentioned.

And so the role of roomscaping is to use the accepted rules of good design for creating house plant arrangements in the same way as we use them in landscaping and flower arranging. In garden landscaping the designer thinks about the various styles (informal, formal, cottage etc) and uses the principles of unity, balance, and so on. Similarly in flower arranging the florist considers style (mass, line etc) and then uses the principles of texture, proportion, movement etc.

And so we shall follow the same route with roomscaping. This chapter begins with an outline of the various house plant features which you can create and then the way you can use the good design principles of balance, unity, contrast, scale, movement etc. A house plant can do so much more than just stand on its own in a plant pot on the sideboard.

Of course, you can enjoy your house plants without being involved in roomscaping. If your interest is solely in the plants and you view the containers as merely vehicles to carry them, then this chapter is not for you. For millions of others, however, there is a real desire to create decorative features with their plants rather than just having them as green pets. This chapter sets out to show the would-be roomscaper how to use house plants in interior design.

THE FEATURE STYLES

THE STAND-ALONE POT

The stand-alone pot houses a foliage or flowering plant which is grown as a solitary feature because of its use or attractive appearance.

page 66

THE POT GROUP

The pot group is a collection of stand-alone pots in which each pot or its holder remains visible.

page 74

THE MULTIPLANT CONTAINER

The multiplant container is a receptacle which contains several plants. No pots are seen — they have been removed or are hidden from sight.

page 82

THE GLASS GARDEN

The glass garden is a feature in which the plants are partially or fully enclosed within a glass container.

page 90

THE WATER GARDEN

The water garden is a feature in which the plants are grown close to or within a water container.

page 96

THE STAND-ALONE POT

The stand-alone pot houses a foliage or flowering plant which is grown as a solitary feature because of its use or attractive appearance.

Some plants (the Specimen Plants) demand to be used on their own — it may be their large size, eye-catching foliage or stunning flowers which warrant this star treatment, and their universal use by interior decorators can be seen in the photographs in any house magazine. But Stand-alone Pots are also used for more workaday purposes — they may be employed to hide unsightly areas or ugly objects (the Cover-up Plants) or they may provide simple, unglamorous green or floral touches in places where there is no room for a group of pots — these are the Accessory Plants.

The Stand-alone Pot is the simplest of all house plant features, and it has a place in every home. Unfortunately, however, it is often the chosen style when it would be better to collect together some or all of the plants to create a Pot Group (page 74) or Multiplant Container (page 82). There really is no place for random pots of fairly ordinary plants dotted around the room if you want them to add to the décor of the room as well as providing you with the satisfaction of growing them. In most cases the standard range of house plants are healthier, more attractive and easier to look after when grouped together.

The solitary pot is unrivalled as a design element when the plant is out of the ordinary and has something to say. There are no competing leaves, flowers or containers to distract the viewer, but this means that there is also nothing to hide imperfect leaves, misshapen branches, poor quality pots etc. Good quality, then, is essential if your plant is to be used as a showpiece in a Stand-alone Pot.

PLANTS TO GROW IN A STAND-ALONE POT

Specimen Plants

A Specimen Plant is one which is best seen standing on its own in a prominent location. The plants which immediately spring to mind are the Architectural Plants described on page 68. These bold members of the house plant world are part of every interior designer's armoury and are frequently used as focal points. A focal point is an item in the room which is attractive or unusual enough to divert attention away from nearby objects. Design experts recommend that focal points should be placed at the middle point of walls and not in corners, but we often find that a corner in the room is the only available area for a bold Architectural Plant.

Having a show plant on the floor and in a corner raises a number of problems. The floor is generally a dark area in a room with standard windows, and a corner can be well away from the source of light. The answer for plants which do not thrive in semi-shady conditions is to move the plant to a bright location for about a week every month.

Not all green foliage plants worthy of a prominent position in a Stand-alone Pot are Architectural Plants. There are small specimens of palms such as Neanthe bella and a wide variety of attractive ferns which can be displayed on furniture or pedestals. In addition there are the many coloured foliage plants like Caladium and Codiaeum which are fine Specimen Plants.

Climbers deserve a special mention, as they are often the least expensive way of obtaining a tall and wide-spreading display. Monstera, the Vines and the Philodendrons are the three ever-popular choices. Most popular trailing plants are excellent mixers and not Specimen Plants, but Chlorophytum is best on its own and so are some of the choice trailers and climbers such as Columnea, Episcia, Hoya etc.

Finally, the flowering house plants. Of course, the spectacular ones in Chapter 7 usually need to be on their own. In addition the showy pot plants are often bold enough to be in Stand-alone Pots — examples are Gloxinia, Poinsettia and Azalea. The virtue of isolation does not belong exclusively to the large-flowering types — plants with masses of small flowers may be best displayed on their own. Bromeliads are another group which benefit from being displayed in Stand-alone Pots — their wide leafy rosettes make them poor bedfellows for other plants.

Cover-up Plants

Here the plant has a practical job to do rather than being a décor feature for the room. The Stand-alone Pot may be placed on the floor, on an item of furniture or be attached to the wall in order to hide ugly features such as exposed pipes or uneven plaster. Large-leaved plants or vigorous climbers are the usual choice.

Accessory Plants

As with the Cover-up Plants these items are not showy enough to add to the beauty of the environment, but are grown on their own instead of as part of a group for one of two reasons. There may not be room for more than a single pot at the chosen site, or it may be special for you like the photograph of a loved one.

Specimen Plants 1 : The Architectural Plant

These members of the Specimen Plant group are sometimes referred to as Decorator Plants in the U.S — a reminder of the important role they play in fashionable room decoration. They are permanent features with year-round interest and so foliage rather than flowering plants are chosen.

The dividing line between Architectural Plants and other Specimen Plants is not a clear-cut one. In simple terms the Architectural ones are free-standing plants which are both attractive and eye-catching because of their shape. Most of them are trees with interesting shapes or spreading leaves. Once the rubber plant was everyone's favourite, but these days you are more likely to see the weeping fig, the fiddle-leaf fig, Dracaena or Yucca.

Boldness is the key, and there are a few rules if you are to get the best out of your Architectural Plant. The background should be plain, and the pot or pot holder should be fairly simple and not too dominant. For a traditional look choose a pot which is about one quarter of the height of the tall plant it contains. As the plant is a focal point, you must keep it in peak condition. Leaves should be dust-free and any yellowing foliage should be removed.

In a contemporary minimalist room the use of a large and striking Architectural Plant is almost an obligatory feature. You might be tempted to start small and grow it on if you want a large plant, but it is usually more satisfactory to buy a plant with the size and shape you require.

Popular Architectural Plants

Araucaria heterophylla
Beaucarnea recurvata
Chamaedorea seifrizii
Cyperus alternifolia
Dicksonia squarrosa
Dracaena fragrans
Dracaena marginata
Ficus benjamina
Ficus elastica decora
Ficus lyrata
Heptapleurum arboricola
Howea belmoreana
Howea forsteriana
Philodendron bipinnatifidum
Phoenix canariensis
Schefflera actinophylla
Sparmannia africana
Yucca elephantipes

Yucca elephantipes

Beaucamea recurvata

Specimen Plants 2 : The Non-architectural Plant

It is a mistake to regard Architectural Plants as the elite of the Specimen Plant group and to treat the remaining plants in the group as being always inferior in size and appeal to their illustrious colleagues.

Every Specimen Plant is worthy of being grown in a Stand-alone Pot for room decoration. The foliage display provided by a mature Monstera deliciosa can be matched by very few Architectural Plants, but it is excluded because it is a climber. An Anthurium or a bird of paradise flower will turn more heads than the average rubber plant or weeping fig, but these floral beauties are not classed as Architectural Plants because their display is not permanent. There are many more examples, including the well-trained bonsai which has a more sculptured look than the average show tree, but it may be too small to join the list of Architectural Plants.

It may be necessary to turn your plant occasionally to prevent lop-sided growth. A word of caution — some flowering plants may drop their buds if the pot is turned.

It should be obvious from this page and the preceding ones that the Stand-alone Pot is an important feature of roomscaping, but it must be stressed once again that the vast range of 'ordinary' foliage plants and small-flowered ones are usually more attractive when grouped together.

Peperomia Lilian

Designer Terms
SCALE

Scale is the relationship of the plant and its container to the size and shape of the room and its furniture — the aim is to ensure that they are in proportion. A tall and spreading palm in a small hall can look hopelessly out of place, whereas a scatter of isolated pots of small plants would spoil the appearance of a large room decorated in a contemporary style.

There are no rules to show how to ensure that the scale is right, but there are guidelines. A floor-standing tree-like plant is the best choice if you are dealing with a large, bare area. Do think big — an average-sized plant may well look lost. A specimen with wide-spreading or drooping leaves will appear to lower the ceiling — a tall, column-like plant will seem to add height to the ceiling.

Don't buy a specimen tree on impulse. Measure the height and width you want to cover before you leave the room, and then take your tape measure to the garden centre to find a plant which will fit the bill.

RECEPTACLES

The confusion over the naming of the various types of units used to hold our house plants has grown worse over the years. The definitions first set out in The House Plant Expert have stood the test of time and so they are maintained here, although the range has continued to grow. The overall term for any type of plant or pot holder is a **receptacle**, and this applies to the whole range of house plant features in this chapter.

Housing the Plant

Pot

The basic feature of a pot is the presence of one or more drainage holes in the base. It may be round, square or any other shape and it may hold one or more plants. If your main interest is the plant rather than its contribution to the décor of the room then you need look no further than the clay or plain plastic pot which was used by the supplier. If on the other hand the receptacle is to be a decorative item then you will have either to choose a more attractive one into which the plant will have to be transplanted or else obtain a pot holder in which you can stand the pot you have bought.

Clay pots have several advantages — they have a 'natural' look and waterlogging is less likely. This is the preferred pot for many experts but it is regarded as too plain for the average roomscaper. Before turning to other materials do remember that ornamental terracotta pots are available. Harmful salts tend to leach on to the surface rather than accumulating in the compost.

Plastic pots are lighter and need watering less often. They come in a wide range of colours and decorative surfaces, which means that a pot holder may not be necessary to create a stylish effect. Foam plastic pots help to prevent overheating on a south-facing windowsill. In recent years semi-transparent pots have become popular for housing orchids.

Glazed Ceramic and Glass pots are not as popular as clay and plastic ones, but they do have their devotees.

+
Drip Tray

This item is essential for placing under a Stand-alone Pot if it is not to be housed in a pot holder. Make sure that it is in keeping with the pot and that it is waterproof — paint the inside with a sealant if in doubt. Place a coaster or other form of drip mat between the drip tray and the carpet or furniture below.

or

Container

The basic feature of this receptacle is that there are no holes in the base. It may be round, square or any other shape and it may hold one or more plants. The virtue of this type of receptacle is that almost any sort of waterproof item can be used. You will find a large variety of containers at your house plant supplier, and many household items continue to serve as house plant containers.

The basic routine is to put a layer of small pebbles or gravel in the bottom and then cover it with a layer of charcoal. The plant is then transplanted into the container in the usual way.

The shape, size and colour of the container can enhance or detract from the beauty of the plant — see the Pot Holder notes on page 71. The wide range is the virtue of the container, but the watering problem is a drawback — see page 112 for details.

Covering the Pot

Pot Holder

The basic features of a pot holder are that the lower part is waterproof and the outer surface adds to the decorative effect of the plant. Size is an important consideration. The ideal width is 5 cm more than the diameter of the top of the pot. The ideal height is a little more than the height of the pot when it is in place — this space should be 1–4 cm, depending on the size of the pot. Stand the pot on a piece of wood or upturned container if it is too small to reach just below the top of the pot holder.

Put a layer of small pebbles or gravel at the base of the pot holder before putting the pot in place. The space between pot and holder can be filled with peat, granulated bark etc to hide the unattractive air space but filling this space is best avoided. The pot has either to be removed for watering and then replaced, or the plant must be watered in its pot holder — the problem with filling the space is that pot removal is not possible and excess water cannot be poured away.

Tastes have changed. In Victorian times the great favourite was the white glazed cachepot with a surface which was often highly decorated. It stood on a pedestal and contained a palm, fern or Aspidistra. Today there is no favourite — it is a matter of personal taste from among the terracotta, ceramic, wood, metal, plastic, glass, cane and glass fibre types which are now available. There are no specific rules for making the right choice but do read the item below on Unity. Do not use a floral pot holder for a flowering plant and do avoid bright colours or strong patterns unless you can trust your design sense. White and black are generally safe bets, and so are a wide range of browns for foliage plants. So as not to clash with the colour of the flowers you should choose an analogous colour for a restful effect or a contrasting colour for a dramatic touch — see the Colour feature on page 94.

Choosing the right size

The only point on which the professional designers agree is that the height of the plant and the height of the pot should not be the same. Extremes should be avoided — the pot must be large enough to prevent the feeling that the plant would blow over in the wind, but small enough not to overwhelm the plant. Having a pot which is between a third and a fifth the height of an Architectural Plant is sometimes quoted as an ideal. The spread of a bushy plant should be between two and three times the width of the pot — for a spreading plant it should be between three and six times the width.

Designer Terms
UNITY

Unity refers to the way designers ensure that various items blend into a harmonious whole. This does not mean that the result should be dull or unexciting. House a blood-red Anthurium in a cylindrical stainless steel container against the stark white wall of a contemporary room and there is all the contrast you could desire — but there is also the unity of modern shapes and surfaces. Again, the shapes, colours and sizes are all different with a small palm in a patterned ceramic pot holder on the piano in a chintzy room — but once again there is unity. There are all sorts of rules which try to help, but the simplest plan is to ask yourself two questions — does the plant seem to belong with the receptacle and does the plant fit in with the room?

THE
STAND-ALONE POT
ILLUSTRATED

A traditional Stand-alone Pot display in a traditional setting — a showy pot plant in front of a not-in-use fireplace to provide a splash of colour for a limited period. ▷

◁ *The Stand-alone Pot usually sits on a sideboard, shelf or table, but a single plant in its pot can be used to clothe a whole wall, provided that the plant choice, position and upkeep are suitable.*

△ *Unlike the azalea above, this bromeliad display has a distinctly 21st century appearance — glass, coloured gravel and sand provide eye-catching alternatives to compost and terracotta.*

A pair of identical Stand-alone Pots can provide interest and a feeling of balance which would be missing from a single pot ▷ display. This point is illustrated by this stair display of paired pitcher plants.

◁ *Metal containers are being used on an increasing scale to replace traditional pots in contemporary settings. This stainless steel pot looks at home in this room, but would be quite wrong in a period room.*

△ *Pot or plant? As a general rule you should aim to have either the pot or the plant as the eye-catching feature. The two photographs above illustrate the point, but this is not an absolute rule and it is sometimes successfully ignored.*

THE POT GROUP

The pot group is a collection of stand-alone pots in which each pot or its holder remains visible.

Pot Group or Stand-alone Pots?

The key feature of the Pot Group is the fact that the plants plus the pots form a single **unit** in which each plant generally has an effect on its neighbours. This can be by reducing light, increasing humidity or by preventing unrestricted growth.

Stand-alone Pots

These three plants are clearly an arrangement of Stand-alone Pots — each one is seen as an individual.

Pot Group

At first glance these three plants are seen as a unit — only later do we see them as individual plants.

It cannot be denied that an outstanding plant deserves a place on its own in a receptacle which does it justice. But the average house plant is not outstanding, and for them the Pot Group offers a number of advantages which are described and illustrated on the following pages.

There are all sorts of ways of bringing a number of pots together. The arrangement can be horizontal or vertical, and the pots may or may not be collected together in some form of open unit such as a wire jardiniere or on a large drip tray. The Victorians were conscious of the value of grouping pots together and there were all sorts of multi-tiered metal units, including the popular corner stand. These pot group stands have lost their charm except as antique pieces, but all the reasons for grouping plants together remain and are listed on pages 76–77. There is an additional advantage which is not listed — the creation of an attractive Pot Group gives the same sort of satisfaction which flower arrangers derive from their work.

The plants can be a restrained collection or a riot of colour — there are no rules but there is guidance on page 75. The grouping and types of pots can range from the very simple to the truly lavish. Obviously, the purpose of creating the Pot Group is to add interest and living colour to part of the room, and advice on the placing of the arrangement is given on pages 78–81.

So now it is up to you. Start to look at the Pot Group as a single unit — that is what you do with your herbaceous border in the garden and your flower arrangement on the sideboard.

CHOOSING THE PLANTS

The Rainbow Group

This is the Pot Group equivalent of the most popular type of flower arrangement — a multi-coloured collection of flowers in front of or within a variety of foliage. Some designers feel that this is too garish a way to use house plants, and it is true that the Rainbow Group is usually a mistake in a room with a complex pattern of bright colours in the carpet, wallpaper, pictures etc. In a plain room, however, using a variety of plain and variegated foliage plants together with brightly-coloured flowering ones can dramatically liven up the scene. To increase the permanence of the display you can use green, variegated and coloured foliage plants without flowering ones.

The Muted Group

Foliage plants dominate this feature. Various types may be used and there may be both ferny and solid-leaved plants, but the basic feature is that green is the prime or only colour. The group can be enlivened by using a variegated plant or two to add a touch of white or yellow, or a flowering plant with white or pastel-coloured blooms may be included, but the effect is always restrained. A Muted Group need not be dull but it is never vibrant. This choice is useful where the Pot Group is to be in front of or close to prominently patterned wallpaper or curtains — it also will have a calming effect when placed near brightly-coloured paintings or other gaudy decorative items.

The Solo Group

Solo grouping is not unusual outdoors — in the garden we have hedges made up of a single species, and blanket bedding using just one type of annual is popular in some European countries. Despite this acceptance outdoors the Pot Group using a single variety is an uncommon sight indoors. Solo planting of a single type of bulb in containers is, of course, one of the most popular of all house plant arrangements, but you rarely see a Pot Group of identical plants. There is an exception — designers are increasingly using this decorative feature in contemporary rooms, as shown in the illustration. The pots are identical and the outline is strictly geometrical.

THE POT GROUP v THE STAND-ALONE POT

The virtue of having an extraordinary plant in a pot on its own rather than being surrounded by others was pointed out on page 66, but in the introduction to this section it was also pointed out that most plants benefit from being grouped together. The four basic reasons are listed on these two pages.

Imperfections can be hidden in a group

The plants we have scattered about the room do tend to suffer as time passes, especially if conditions are not quite right. The lower leaves of some types such as Croton may have fallen because the air is too dry, and the scorched leaf tips of palms and dumb canes caused by too much sun have to be removed. In addition there is the unattractive appearance of a small flower-head on a long stalk and the unbalanced effect of a plant which is lop-sided. These defects, and others, are unavoidable — the answer is to collect the plants together into a Pot Group in which the bare stems, trimmed leaves and long flower stalks are hidden.

Bare-stemmed Croton and lop-sided rose, begonia, palm and goosefoot plant.

An attractive Pot Group is created when they are packed together.

Plants usually thrive better in a group

It has been found that many plants benefit from being placed next to others in a group rather than being grown in isolation. The usual explanation is that they benefit from the increase in humidity which is found in this microclimate — this extra humidity arises from the evaporation of the moisture from the newly misted leaves and the damp compost in the surrounding pots. This increase in humidity results in a reduction in the shrivelling of the leaves of moisture-lovers such as the delicate ferns. In addition the general vigour of the plant is sometimes increased, and the reasons are not fully known.

The leaflets on the maidenhair ferns in the centre of the Pot Group have remained fresh and green.

The edges of the leaflets on a fern in a Stand-alone Pot tend to shrivel in the dry air in winter.

Plants are easier to care for in a group

The ritual of looking after a number of plants scattered around the room involves moving from plant to plant in order to water or mist — it is of course an easier task to pour on water from a watering can and moisten the leaves with a mister when the plants are collected together in a Pot Group. This virtue is the one cited as the cultural benefit of grouping the pots together, but the amount of effort saved is not usually significant. A point which is not mentioned is that weak stems, lop-sided growth and flopping flower-heads call for the job of staking with plants in Stand-alone Pots — when grown in a group these wayward stems and stalks can often be supported by their taller neighbours. In addition the task of trimming brown leaf tips and minor imperfections is much less necessary in a leafy group with a variety of colours and textures.

Plants usually look better in a group

A Specimen Plant (page 67) can be grown on its own in a Stand-alone Pot or as part of a group in a Pot Group or a Multiplant Container. As part of a group it can serve as a sole or joint focal point, providing a centre of interest to the collection. Most small-leaved and low-growing plants do not have this degree of visual appeal. When grown in a Stand-alone Pot they may look quite insignificant, but in a group they take on two functions which add considerably to the visual appeal of the group. Firstly, they add greenery of various textures between and in front of the Specimen Plants, and the blooms of quite modest flowering plants can add dramatically to the display. Secondly, trailers such as ivy and creeping fig become features of interest when used to soften the front edge of the Pot Group or Multiplant Container.

Designer Terms
CONTRAST

Unity (page 71) and Contrast would seem to be opposing design ideas, but they are not. Unity means that the plant feature should fit in with the overall appearance of the room — there should never be a feeling that it doesn't belong. Within the plant/container/ background combination, however, there should be some degree of contrast. This means that there should be a marked difference between one or more of these items. The degree of contrast between the plant(s) and the receptacle(s) is a matter of personal taste, but there are some points to remember. A green plant in a green pot can look boringly dull, but the use of a brightly-coloured or highly-patterned container will take attention away from the plant. Although there need not be a high degree of contrast between plant and pot there should be clear-cut contrast between the plant feature and its background. A Rainbow Group (page 75) certainly looks best against a plain background — white is ideal, but other pastel shades will do. Putting a Rainbow Group in front of a highly-patterned multi-coloured background is a design fault. Against such paper or curtains you should choose a display in which large green leaves predominate.

POT GROUP DISPLAYS
The Standard Group

A Standard Pot Group is a collection of plants in individual pots or containers which are placed closely together. To make a Pot Group which has that 'interior decorator' look calls for a knowledge of the principles of good design, and here there is a problem. For flower arrangers there are scores of instruction manuals, flower clubs and videos, but there is virtually no guidance for the house plant arranger. Of course you may have a good sense of design and you may be an old hand at roomscaping, but for the rest a few words of advice should be useful.

First of all, study the explanation of the Designer Terms which you will find in this chapter. The next step is to buy your plants, and here there are several factors to bear in mind. Choose three or a larger odd number. They should all have rather similar light and temperature needs. Next, there should be a range of heights and textures, but a wide range of pot types is generally not a good idea. The usual choice is a selection of foliage plants to provide the permanent skeleton and some flowering ones to provide a temporary colourful display. Many designers use only foliage ones and rely on differences in size, leaf texture and colour to give variety to the arrangement. Good displays can be created either way — it is up to you.

Be careful with the pots. Too much variety of colour, shape and size can confuse the picture if you are not an expert — it is usually preferable to have pots which are rather similar and with drip trays which do not draw attention to themselves.

And now for the arrangement. If the Pot Group is to be viewed from only the front and sides, then have the taller plants at the back, the smaller ones at the front, and intermediate ones in the middle. This is an overall concept which must not be slavishly followed. A straight line look must be avoided — reduce the back row height at the sides and do have ups and downs to give a feeling of movement. The tall plants at the back are usually bold-leaved foliage types with the flowering ones closer to the front, but once again this is not a rule. Outline shape is a matter of personal taste — the lop-sided pyramid is popular.

The basic plan for an arrangement which is to be viewed from all sides is to have the taller plants in the middle with the smaller ones surrounding them. Once again you must break up this overall pattern to ensure movement — see page 79. With a corner arrangement the tallest plant is the innermost one and the smaller plants are set on either side.

The De-luxe Pot Group

Compared with the Standard Pot Group there are often fewer and not more plants in the De-luxe version. The plants need not be more unusual nor more impressive. The key difference between the two is that the appearance of the pots is important in the De-luxe Pot Group — it is a plant plus pot display. The pots are of different sizes and both their shape and material are eye-catching and sometimes unusual. The large pots are at the rear, and there is usually a marked difference in height from the flowers at the front to the bold foliage at the back. For the modern interior designer the plants are only part of the Pot Group display.

The Pebble Tray

The Pebble Tray is the answer to so many problems, and yet it remains a rare sight. The worry about overwatering and emptying drip trays becomes a thing of the past — excess water runs into the gravel. Maintaining a moist atmosphere becomes much easier — water around the gravel is constantly evaporating into the microclimate around the plants. Any waterproof shallow container will do provided it can hold a 3–5 cm layer of gravel. Arrange the Pot Group on the surface and keep the water level about halfway up the gravel layer — do not have standing water on the surface. It is a great home for difficult plants.

Designer Terms
MOVEMENT

Movement is a simple concept which is easy to understand — it is any technique or material which moves the eye from one part of the display to another. The first thing to do is to make sure that two or more of the plants you buy for a group display are eye-catching enough to serve as focal points — these are areas to which the eye is drawn and rests there for a little time. Focal points should be separated in the arrangement. Next, aim for what flower arrangers call 'ins and outs' — the flowers/leaves should not create a level surface over a large area. Curves are very important — note how the trailing plant in the arrangement on the right moves the eye from one feature to the other. There is a final golden rule. One plant should not be so dominant as to distract the eye for a long time from the other plants in the group — use such a Specimen Plant in a Stand-alone Pot.

THE POT GROUP ILLUSTRATED

One of the most popular types of Pot Group — a cluster of containers on the hearth to hide a fireplace. The flowering pot plants add colour to a dull area. ▷

◁ A variety of plants and pots is not essential. This grouping of identical white Kalanchoes provides an eye-catching feature in this contemporary-style room.

△ An opposite approach to the white pots above — a mixture of pots and a riot of foliage colour make up this corner arrangement. Note the central focus plant.

An example of the way house plants can transform a room. Two groups of Stand-alone Pots containing Strelitzias provide colour and a dramatic touch. ▷

◁ A Pot Group which differs markedly from the arrangement above. The mixed collection forms a colourful mass, but in both cases the pots are hidden.

△ A classical springtime Pot Group — hyacinths, daffodils and cyclamen promise things to come in the garden outside the window. Here the containers are an important feature.

THE MULTIPLANT CONTAINER

The multiplant container is a receptacle which contains several plants. No pots are seen — they have been removed or are hidden from sight.

Like the Pot Group this feature brings plants together rather than leaving them dotted round the room. There are similarities between them — imperfections can be hidden, air humidity around the leaves is increased and watering is easier when the plants are not isolated. As noted later, however, there are distinct advantages and disadvantages with these two methods of bringing plants together.

The Multiplant Container is a receptacle in which two or more plants are grown, but unlike the Pot Group no pots or containers are visible. The plants have either been taken out of their pots and transplanted into the container or else the pots have been surrounded up to their rims with peat, coir, bark chippings or compost.

The basic advantage of this feature compared with the Pot Group is that you are truly gardening. Instead of arranging pots you are putting together a mini-garden as you do outdoors with a windowbox, container or flower bed. In addition to the added pleasure of putting the plants together in a planter there is a feeling of 'oneness' about the display which many people find satisfying. One other advantage — the compost around the pots acts as an insulator against the cold of the unheated room in winter and the baking sun on a south-facing windowsill.

There are also disadvantages compared with the Pot Group. It is easy to overwater as there is no drip tray to catch the excess when plants are kept in their pots, and matters are worse when the plants are grown in the compost of the container. The plants cannot be turned to prevent lop-sided growth and removal is not easy when one has to be replaced. Another drawback is that really tall plants are not suitable for an ordinary planter. Still, there is something special about a Multiplant Container and they should certainly be more popular. Whatever your circumstances there is one for you as they range in size from tiny dishes to large beds in conservatories.

MULTIPLANT CONTAINER DISPLAYS
The Mixed Bowl

The Mixed Bowl is one of the most popular of all Multiplant Container types. It is nearly always bought ready-planted from a super-market, garden centre or DIY superstore for standing on the sideboard or for giving as a present. The usual receptacle is a round bowl but any small waterproof container can be used. Receptacles may vary but there is a standard planting pattern. The simplest version is shown in the photograph — a tall plant (variegated ivy) is set at the back of the bowl and a bushy or spreading foliage plant (maidenhair fern) is planted below together with a flowering type (flaming katy). A trailing plant (creeping fig) is grown close to the front to soften the edge of the bowl. More than one plant may be used at any of these stations, but the same general pattern remains. Watering is a major problem. The container is usually shallow and there are generally no drainage holes, so overwatering is difficult to avoid.

If you are starting from scratch it is better to use a receptacle with drainage holes at the bottom and to add a layer of gravel before adding the compost and planting. Stand the bowl on a drip tray.

The Mixed Bowl is often criticised because it is not a permanent display — the stage is quite quickly reached when it becomes overcrowded. However, it lasts much longer than a flower arrangement and the plants can be removed and used in another house plant feature.

Designer Terms
BALANCE

There are two aspects to the concept of balance. The first one concerns the plant or plants in the receptacle. Here there must be physical balance, which means that the receptacle and its compost must be heavy enough to prevent a one-sided arrangement from toppling over. In addition there must also be visual balance, which means that a physically-stable feature must not *look* as if it could topple over. You can increase the 'weight' of the lighter side of a visually-unbalanced feature by introducing plants with large, dark leaves. The second aspect of balance concerns the visual impact of two nearby features, which may be quite different in style, against a wall. To see if they are balanced, imagine them on the pans of a giant pair of scales — if one side would clearly outweigh the other then the effect is not balanced.

The Standard Planter

This house plant feature differs from the Mixed Bowl by generally containing a wider range of plants and by having them retained in their pots rather than in compost within the container. A Planter is usually easier to maintain and usually more attractive to look at than its smaller counterpart, so for most situations this is the Multiplant Container to choose.

The Planter you are most likely to be offered is a plain plastic oblong trough in white, black, green or brown. Thoroughly workman-like, but not a design feature and it is worth looking further afield if you are roomscaping. Wood and cane are better surfaces for a period room and polished steel may be ideal for a contemporary one. A square or a wide circular Planter offers more scope than the long rectangle, and you don't have to rely on the shop-bought version. You can use any waterproof container which is slightly higher than the tallest pots it will house when they are stood on the gravel layer. The experts advise against a patterned or over-colourful surface which can detract from or compete with the plant display.

Place a 3–5 cm layer of gravel on the base to serve as a soakaway — on top of this layer stand the pots. Clay pots are preferred —

they must have drainage holes. The tallest pots can be stood on a thin layer of packing material placed on top of the soakaway — smaller pots will need some form of support to bring them to a little below the rim of the Planter. It may be necessary to stand a small pot on an upturned empty one.

You have now reached the final stage, which is the addition of the packing layer of peat or compost. Before you start insert the water gauge — see below. Add the damp packing layer so that it completely fills the space between the soakaway and the rim of the pots. Do not add this packing layer around the stems of plants in lowly-placed pots — raise them as described above.

Take care when watering and keep the packing layer damp but not wet. This layer increases the humidity of the air around the plants and may act as a source of moisture if the roots are allowed to grow through the drainage holes of the pot and into the packing layer. You will find that the plants in a Planter require watering less frequently than those in Stand-alone Pots.

Watch for pests and diseases — the close planting in this type of feature increases the risk of attack. Prune as necessary and remove dead plants promptly.

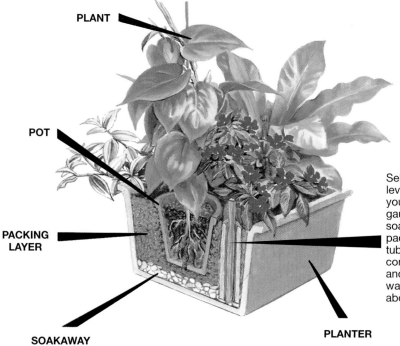

PLANT

POT

PACKING LAYER

SOAKAWAY

PLANTER

WATER GAUGE
Self-watering troughs with water-level indicators are available, but you can build your own water gauge. Insert a tube through the soakaway layer before adding the packing layer — the base of the tube should touch the bottom of the container. Insert a stick in the tube and use it as a dipstick — the water level should not reach above the top of the soakaway.

Planting-up the Planter

The first consideration is to look for plants which have roughly the same requirements — not exactly the same, but it would be foolish to expect succulents and ferns to grow happily together. When deciding what to buy, do remember that a mid-sized plant beneath a large and spreading pinnacle one will receive less light than a similar plant growing in a Stand-alone Pot. Next, think of the types you will need. The usual plan is to have one or more tall pinnacle plants, a number of mid-sized ones and then a few creeping and spreading ones to clothe a part of the Planter edge. The standard approach is to have a permanent skeleton of foliage plants. Pinnacle and mid-sized varieties give the basic shape to the display and small-leaved types are used at the front to soften the rim — both plain green and variegated plants are employed. Flowering types are used within this framework to add colour.

Choose a mixture of shapes and textures and avoid the pitfall of trying to use too many — you should allow the larger plants to display their beauty without being crushed by others. There are variations to the standard plan — you could use coloured foliage plants instead of flowering ones or you could display a single foliage species in an ultra-modern setting. To help you with your arrangement read the sections on Contrast (page 77), Movement (page 79), Shape, Texture & Pattern (page 87) and pages 75 and 78 in the Pot Group section.

An arrangement incorporating a number of good design features — there are movement, balance, and marked contrasts in texture and shape.

An arrangement with a flower arranger's touch — Fittonia and Philodendron nestle beneath a piece of driftwood.

A rainbow arrangement of foliage and flowers in an overly-bright bowl. For most situations a more muted container would have been preferable.

The Pot-et-Fleur

This type of Multiplant Container is a combination of arranging house plants and flower arranging — it is basically a Standard Planter. A cylindrical or square container is planted up in the usual way — see page 85 for instructions. The only difference is that a deep glass or metal tube is pushed into the compost in front of the tallest pinnacle plant and between adjacent mid-sized foliage plants. Cut flowers are then put into the water-filled tube, and this is where there may be some confusion. This house plant feature is not the place for a flower arrangement — it is the place to display one or more eye-catching blooms which can serve as a focal point. The Pot-et-Fleur is just a Multiplant Container with a special touch.

The De-luxe Planter

This feature may be no larger than the Standard Planter (page 84) and its planting and arrangement need not be on a grander scale. The difference is that the De-luxe Planter is made up of two or more planters which may be part of a single unit or a number of square, rectangular or round planters pushed tightly together. The planters are carefully chosen to have maximum appeal and there is nearly always a marked difference in height. Ready-made models are available or you could buy separate planters and stand them together. You can build your own with plastic-coated board if you are a DIY enthusiast — make sure all joints are sealed. A De-luxe Planter will allow you to use your design sense to the full. The tallest planter is usually used for a large Architectural Plant. At its base one or more low-growing spreading plants can be used and one of the Planters can be used for seasonal bedding such as bulbs in spring and Poinsettias at Christmas time.

The Hanging Basket

Most cascading plants have to be seen at eye-level or above in order for their beauty to be fully appreciated. The pots can be stood on a pedestal or high shelf, but a Hanging Basket is the answer if you want to create a feature which will provide interest and colour to the upper part of a room. In front of a window where the view is not vital is a favourite site, so is a long bare wall where a bracketed support is used to hold the container. Two types are available. There is the waterproof Standard Planter with chains attached and there is also the plastic bowl-shaped basket with built-in drip tray. Look for a fixing ring which rotates so that you can turn the basket to ensure even growth.

The fixing to the ceiling or on the wall must be secure. Use plants growing in soilless compost and surround the pots with moist peat. Hanging Baskets must not be neglected — the air near the ceiling is warmer than elsewhere, there may be less light and more frequent watering will be necessary. The easiest way to water is to instal a pulley fitting so that the basket can be pulled down — alternatively lift it off the hook each time you need to water, or buy a pump-action watering can. Don't restrict your choice to ordinary hanging plants like ivy and creeping fig — do include one or more flowering cascade types such as Begonia, Columnea, Episcia and Fuchsia.

Designer Terms
SHAPE, TEXTURE & PATTERN

These terms are used to describe the appearance of the foliage of a house plant. Shape covers the size and outline of the leaf, Texture is the physical nature of its surface and Pattern is the distribution of colour. Wander around the display at a large garden centre to see the range of Shapes — tiny-leaved mind-your-own-business to 50 cm-wide Monstera leaves, straight-edged Crotons to feathery asparagus fern. The range of Textures is equally wide — smooth, spiny, dull, shiny, velvety, ruffled etc. Finally, the patterns — all-green, variegated (green plus one other colour), multi-coloured, veined and so on. A mixture of Shapes, Patterns and Textures in your display will add interest, but a word of caution is necessary — too many different types in a feature can lead to confusion.

The Built-in Planter

The Built-in Planter is the ultimate house plant feature — here we bring a garden bed indoors. In the home it is nearly always found in a conservatory or garden room — in offices and public buildings it is usually constructed in the foyer. The most satisfactory type of Built-in Planter is made at the same time as the building — it is a ground floor feature which contains soil or compost in the same way as the border in the greenhouse.

This type of Built-in Planter is, of course, out of the question once the house is built, but if the space available and the environment are right you can construct a raised bed if the foundation below is sound. You will need a retaining wall of brick, reconstituted stone, wood or tile-covered blocks which will hold a 10 cm layer of gravel and a 40 cm layer of compost — paint the inside with bituminous paint before filling.

Location is important. You will need a large area — the conservatory is ideal but a large hallway can also be considered. Good light is essential — do not think of constructing a built-in garden if there is not glass overhead or a large window alongside. The usual routine is to plant out the large foliage plants and other permanent specimens and then to add temporary flowering plants — keep these in their pots so as to facilitate easy removal. The addition of a water feature and hidden lighting will turn a Built-in Planter into an outstanding focal point in any spacious location, but would be quite out of place in an average-sized room.

The Dish Garden

This house plant feature is at the other end of the scale from the Built-in Planter — it can be one of the smallest of the Multiplant Containers. Small perhaps, but it is not easy to construct a really attractive one. You will need a shallow dish with a layer of gravel and charcoal at the bottom if it does not have drainage holes — fill to near the rim with soilless compost. A number of succulents are then used to landscape the dish following the general guidance on page 85. Use a tree-like specimen such as Crassula argentea as the pinnacle plant and then some smaller types to fill the space around — grow one or more trailers such as Senecio rowleyanus close to the rim. Aim for a range of shapes and colours — cacti can be included. Stand on a windowsill — do not overwater.

THE MULTIPLANT CONTAINER ILLUSTRATED

Two black planters make up this office feature. A range of tough foliage plants have been used — flowering pot plants have been excluded so as to ensure easy maintenance. ▷

◁ *A simple box Planter for the sitting room. The wide variety of shapes, colours and textures of the foliage rather than the container surface provides the interest.*

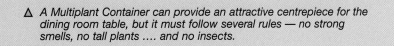

△ *A Multiplant Container can provide an attractive centrepiece for the dining room table, but it must follow several rules — no strong smells, no tall plants .... and no insects.*

THE GLASS GARDEN

The glass garden is a feature
in which the plants are partially or
fully enclosed within a glass container.

A Glass Garden is a rare sight in the house these days, but it was not always so. The early Victorians were passionate about foliage plants in the parlour, but the range of varieties they could grow was limited — they were restricted to Aspidistra, Kentia, Nephrolepis and other tough types which could withstand the smoke-filled air in the 19th century house.

It all changed with the work of Dr Nathaniel Ward. In 1829 this London doctor had accidentally discovered that delicate ferns thrived in a sealed jar and did not need watering. The Wardian Case was born, and plants were shipped round the world with very few losses inside these miniature greenhouses.

These cases were put to good use in the home. Glass-sided boxes (renamed Fern Cases) became a familiar sight in Victorian homes and a wide variety of shapes and sizes was offered by department stores and home shopping catalogues. Alongside them in the stores and catalogues were the small window conservatories (see page 93) but with the arrival of the 20th century this enthusiasm for the Glass Garden began to wane. In the U.K it was the planted-up Carboy which kept alive the interest in the Glass Garden.

Growing plants in glass in today's home has a number of virtues, even though protection from smoke-laden air is no longer needed. The air around the leaves is kept moist and the plants are not affected by draughts. An important additional benefit is that plants in a closed Glass Garden will rarely need to be watered.

All sorts of household items and custom-made containers can be used, as shown on the following pages. Choose glass — transparent plastic is less satisfactory. Pick your plants carefully — avoid quick-growing ones as space is usually limited and flowering ones should be avoided when stocking a Bottle Garden. Also avoid plants which need dry air or good air circulation. Do take the opportunity to grow some of the difficult tropical ones which need still, moist air and do not thrive under ordinary room conditions — see page 94 for suggestions.

Your Glass Garden will certainly arouse interest and will also give you the pleasure of growing unusual varieties, but it cannot be expected to add to the general decor of the room — that is the job of the other groups in this chapter.

The Bottle Garden

For a period in the middle of the 20th century the Bottle Garden became a popular feature — large carboys which had once been used to transport chemicals were in great demand. Every house plant textbook had to have its how-to-do-it page on this novel way to grow house plants. The main attraction was the promise that there was no need to ever water again.

The basic feature of a Bottle Garden is that the opening in the container is restricted. The difficulty involved in planting and upkeep increases as the size of the opening decreases and the height of the bottle increases. You can make life easy by choosing a bottle you can get your hand in — a narrow-necked bottle such as a carboy means that you will need to make a few tools and use some skill. The opening on the Bottle Garden need not be at the top — a tall square bottle can be placed on its side for filling, planting and display.

Use a clean and dry bottle. If the bottle is large it is a good idea to pour in a 5 cm layer of gravel which is then covered with a thin layer of charcoal — this stage can be omitted if you are using a small container. To add this gravel and charcoal layer (plus the compost at a later stage), you will need to use a funnel of rolled-up cardboard pushed into the opening — this will keep the materials off the side of the glass.

You will need a 5–8 cm layer of moist soilless compost. Tamp this down with a cotton reel at the end of a cane and landscape it to form a slope if you wish.

Now it's planting time, and you should have given some careful thought to the selection of specimens. There are three rules you should follow. First of all, pick plants which are suitable for a Glass Garden — these are slow-growing foliage plants and the popular ones are listed on page 94. Next choose small specimens — generally the smallest pots you can find. Finally, avoid flowering varieties if the opening is too small for you to reach in with your hand.

The planter tools are a fork and spoon, each attached to a cane. Remove the pots from each plant and use the tools to insert the rootballs into the compost. Firm each one into the growing medium and press down with the cotton-reel tamper.

Some people add a thin layer of decorative stones or fine sand over the surface, but this is not necessary. Again, pouring a little water down the side of the glass is sometimes recommended, but should not be necessary if the compost was damp and the sides are clean. You must be careful to avoid overwatering.

Place the Bottle Garden in a spot where it is reasonably bright but which receives no direct sunlight. A low table is a popular place — turning it into a base for a table lamp is a concept which professional roomscapers find unacceptable.

You will need a stopper. If one isn't available you can cover the top with cling film. Leave the opening uncovered until the mist on the side has cleared — once it has gone the top should be sealed with the stopper or film. Your Bottle Garden should now look after itself, although misting of the glass may be a problem — see page 94.

One final recommendation. The how-did-you-get-the-plant-in-the-bottle effect may arouse interest, but it really is a poor way of growing house plants — the Terrarium described on page 92 is a much better idea.

The Terrarium

The one advantage that the Terrarium has over the Bottle Garden is that you can use your hand for planting and then use it again for removing items which have to be replaced. The shop-bought Terrarium is a version of the original Wardian Case illustrated on page 90. It opens at the side and it should be filled with gravel, charcoal and compost as described for the Bottle Garden.

You can make your own Terrarium from a fishtank, as illustrated below. Landscape the 'ground' with hills and valleys if you wish, and plant small specimens of suitable varieties — see page 94. Do not put them too close together. You can use flowering plants, but keep them in their pots so that you can easily remove them when the blooms have faded. When you have finished place a sheet of bevelled glass over the top and choose a bright but sunless spot.

Looking after a fishtank Terrarium is a simple matter, and so is the aftercare of the shop-bought version if it is fully glazed. Most of them, however, are only partly glazed and so one of the main advantages of the Glass Garden is lost — you will have to water every few weeks not every few months or years. See page 94 for guidance on how to look after your Glass Garden.

The Plant Window

This is a hybrid of a small conservatory and the Glass Gardens described on earlier pages. Like the Terrarium it has glass on all sides, but it is usually larger and is attached to the house rather than being placed on a stand or table. The Plant Window offers much more scope than a small Terrarium, but the air may not be as moist and more frequent watering will be necessary.

It is essentially an external window with glass above and at the sides, and an internal glazed door or window which provides access. The Plant Window has acquired a number of names over the years — window conservatory, window garden, reach-in greenhouse etc and it has a long history. All sorts of designs, shapes and sizes have been produced. These range from the simple window attachments which were widely offered in Victorian and Edwardian home improvement catalogues to the substantial floor-to-ceiling mini-conservatories which are occasionally built into some houses at the present time. Examples of both are shown here but you will very rarely see a Plant Window in Britain. There was no interest in this form of room addition in Britain after World War I, although it has remained a feature in some homes in the U.S and Continental Europe.

The shop-bought window conservatories of the 19th century are a thing of the past in modern Britain, but aluminium versions with various refinements are available in the U.S. This lack of off-the-shelf models means that home carpentry or calling in a builder is the only answer for the keen British house plant grower who wants to create this environment. An existing window is replaced by a glass-sided and glass-roofed structure which has glazed doors opening into the room. The base is usually about 60 cm wide and should be covered with a pebble tray — see page 79. Overheating can be a major problem in summer. Opening the doors or lifting the window at the front will help, but both ventilators and some form of shading are necessary. Shelving is often installed to increase the plant-holding capacity, but rows of pots means that the visual appeal of creating a jungle in the Plant Window is lost. Another optional extra is a small heater to keep the plants from being chilled in icy weather.

Make sure the foliage is kept off the glass so as to avoid damage from scorching sun in summer and ice-cold glass in winter.

19th century Plant Window

21st century Plant Window

TAKING CARE OF YOUR GLASS GARDEN

The moisture in the compost in your Bottle Garden or Terrarium is just right if the plants are healthy and the glass only mists up on cold nights. If water condenses on the sides during the day you should remove the stopper, lift the lid or leave the door slightly open until it disappears. Be careful not to overwater — see below. If condensation on the cover of a fishtank is a problem, then prop up one end of the cover slightly to stop drips falling onto the leaves below.

Water with care. A completely enclosed system can usually carry on for at least several months without watering being necessary. In a partially enclosed system you will have to feel the compost from time to time — watering may be necessary every 2–4 weeks.

Keep growth in check by pruning — remember to remove dead and diseased stems. You will need a blade attached to a cane to prune plants in a Bottle Garden.

PLANTS FOR YOUR GLASS GARDEN

Croton
Fittonia
Maranta
Cryptanthus
Rhoeo
Selaginella
Calathea
Small Ferns
Small-leaved Hedera
Pellionia
Peperomia
Pilea
Saxifraga sarmentosa
Begonia rex
Hypoestes
Ficus pumila
Small Araucaria
Small Neanthe
Episcia
Small Syngonium
Plectranthus

Designer Terms HUE, TINT & SHADE

THE WARM COLOURS
The warm colours brighten up the display. The hues are often dramatic and direct the eye away from the cool colours — the tints and shades are more subdued.

WHITE
White on its own has a calming effect — when placed next to warm colours the result is to make them look brighter.

THE COOL COLOURS
The cool colours quieten down the display. The hues are restful and provide an air of tranquility, but they are overshadowed by bright warm colours.

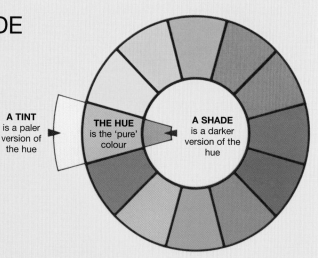

A TINT is a paler version of the hue

THE HUE is the 'pure' colour

A SHADE is a darker version of the hue

MONOCHROMATIC DISPLAY
In a monochromatic scheme the various tints and shades of a single hue are the colours of the flowers and/or the non-green parts of the leaves.

ANALOGOUS DISPLAY
In an analogous scheme the two, three or four hues of the flowers and/or the non-green parts of the leaves are all neighbours on the colour wheel.

CONTRASTING DISPLAY
In a contrasting scheme the two hues of the flowers and/or the non-green parts of the leaves are directly opposite on the colour wheel.

POLYCHROMATIC DISPLAY
In a polychromatic (or rainbow) scheme the hues of the flowers and/or the non-green parts of the leaves are from all parts of the wheel.

THE GLASS GARDEN ILLUSTRATED

All sorts of bottle shapes and sizes have been used to create glass gardens. Remember that difficulty increases as the size of opening decreases. ▷

◁ *A collection of ferns planted in a Victorian fern case. The Fern Craze was at its height in the 1860s — one catalogue listed 818 species.*

△ *The large carboy garden was once popular, but not any more. The reason is that putting in the plants is difficult and so is trying to remove unwanted growth.*

△ *Carnivorous plants are an excellent choice for the terrarium, especially if companion planting is used to create a tropical feel.*

THE WATER GARDEN

The water garden is a feature in which the plants are grown close to or within a water container.

Until recently water was hardly ever seen as a decorative feature in the home, but in recent years a variety of simple table-top fountains and waterfalls have appeared — the tinkling sound of moving water is there, but plants are not.

There must be a good reason for our failure to put plants and water together indoors. It cannot be a lack of interest in water gardening — the small plant-filled pond is one of the fastest-growing features in outdoor gardening. Nor can it be the price — the cost of one of these indoor waterfalls is less than a meal for two. Finally, it cannot be a shortage of advantages — unlike its out-door counterpart this feature helps nearby plants by increasing humidity and it pro-vides a novelty item to impress your friends.

The basic reason would seem to be that unlike garden ponds it has been denied the magic of the TV makeover and there has been virtually nothing in the magazines. Interest in indoor water gardening is increasing in the U.S — the problem in Britain is that so many of our experts believe that growing water plants indoors is not practical. Here is your chance to prove they are wrong.

The photographs on this page illustrate the range of Water Gardens. The feature can be as small as a simple bowl with a single water plant or it may be as large as the colourful conservatory jungle complete with waterfall shown at the bottom of the page. There is every size and shape in between, but they all fall into just two groups — the In-water Display and the Around-water Display.

THE AROUND-WATER DISPLAY

Ordinary house plants and not aquatic ones are used here — they are grown in pots or containers around a water feature. It is possible to incorporate a water feature (page 98) within a Multiplant Container (pages 82–89) — these displays are becoming increasingly popular in the U.S. However, ready-made units are not available, and a simpler approach is to create a Pot Group Water Garden. The starting point is a shop-bought water feature which will have some form of moving water — a small fountain, a round bubble jet, a rock waterfall or a series of water-filled jars is the usual choice. Place it on a firm surface and have a light source which highlights the moving water.

Now place the plants in their pots around the water feature. Many of the points raised in the Pot Group section (pages 74–81) apply, but there are special rules for arrangement. The tallest plants should be at the back of the display — the mid-sized ones should be at the sides to enclose the water area. A weeping plant which does not interfere with the fountain or waterfall is an effective addition. Low-growing plants and trailers belong at the front — try to hide the edge of the water container.

Designer Terms
THE GOLDEN RATIO

This term is used by designers to describe the ratio 1 to 1.618 — it has been used since the time of Ancient Greece to create visually pleasing effects in buildings, paintings, landscaping, room design etc. About 2500 years ago it was found that this ratio was the basis of many of the proportions found in the human body, and later it was found that it applied to flowers, trees, shells and so on. And so it was applied to art — the relationship of the width to the length of the Parthenon in Athens follows the Golden Ratio, and so do many of the features in paintings from the 14th to the 21st century.

In roomscaping we can use a simplified version of this formula, which has been given many names including the Golden Mean, Golden Rectangle, Divine Proportion and the Golden Section. In simple terms it means that if a plant is 1½ times taller than its neighbour, then the effect will be pleasing to our inner designer eye. If you are covering an area of wall with plants, try to aim for a rectangle with one side 1½ times longer than the other. This is sometimes called the Goldilocks effect because of its not-too-little, not-too-much feel, but it is not a Golden Rule. There are times when a much more dramatic ratio is preferable.

THE IN-WATER DISPLAY

In this display one or more aquatic plants are grown in the water — ordinary house plants may or may not be kept nearby. Quite simply, this is a matter of bringing the garden pond indoors. The pleasure of having water lilies growing indoors is of course the main attraction of having an In-water Display of plants. Most experts feel that growing aquatics in the home is not practical, and the idea is rarely mentioned in house plant books. It was not always so — water gardens in the parlour were features in many Victorian houses, and for some the plants rather than the fish were the main attraction.

The critics are right to raise the drawbacks. Good light is absolutely essential. A glass-roofed conservatory is ideal but a raised area near a south-facing window should be satisfactory. Pond balance which keeps the water naturally clear outdoors does not occur indoors — the water area is too small and the temperature of the water is higher than in the garden. Finally, two outdoor features should be omitted from the In-water Display of plants if you want to grow water lilies — fish and water-moving features such as fountains and waterfalls have no place here.

Despite these drawbacks it is worth trying this novel approach to growing plants indoors if you like a challenge. Even if water lilies do not succeed there are other attractive aquatics which will grow in quite shady conditions.

The first job is to choose the most suitable type and size. There is an enormous range from small glass bowls to large sunken pools, but the two which can be most strongly recommended are the half-barrel Minipond for the sunny living room and the Conservatory Pond for the glazed plant room.

The Minipond

Any container which will hold at least 25 litres of water can be used as long as it is decorative, waterproof, non-corrosive and non-toxic. It should also be deep enough to allow the water level to be at least 15 cm above the top of the plant baskets. Deep troughs, large bowls, fibreglass tanks etc can be used but perhaps the most attractive choice is a half-barrel which you can buy from your local garden centre. You can start work between May and September. Varnish the outside and treat the inside with bitumen paint or alternative sealant. Place the container on a firm surface in the brightest spot available.

The next task is to add tap water and then wait for at least three days before you begin planting. You will need a dwarf water lily plus some floaters and oxygenators to help to suppress algal growth. It is essential to have a good cover of leaves — some floaters can be removed when the water lily pads start to spread. There may be room for a marginal plant — see page 100 for advice on plants and planting.

The Conservatory Pond

A Conservatory Pond can be a simple structure for water lilies as shown below or a colourful showpiece with waterfall, lighting, a range of aquatics inside and a collection of house plants outside — see page 101.

The basic requirements are a sound base, a fully waterproof inner surface and a water level which is deep enough for the chosen plants. The inclusion of fish is not a good idea, nor is a fountain or waterfall if you plan to grow water lilies.

Illustrated on the right are the three methods of construction. The simplest plan is to buy a rigid liner and cover the sides with wooden panels or wood roll. A brick, block or reconstituted stone pond looks more substantial — brick and block walls can be tiled to improve their appearance. You may wish to instal a filtration system at this stage in order to keep the water clear.

Fill with tap water and leave for three days before planting — the minimum depth required will depend on the plants which are to be grown. Your aim should be to keep about two-thirds of the surface covered with water lilies and/or floaters so as to suppress the development of green algae. Cleaning out the pond by siphoning out the water may be necessary every five years. Keep plants in buckets of water while this work is being undertaken.

Two words of warning. Employ an electrician if you plan to instal a fountain or waterfall. Secondly, remember that an active toddler can drown in 10 cm of water.

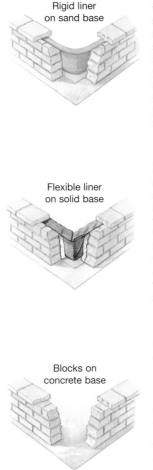

Rigid liner
on sand base

Flexible liner
on solid base

Blocks on
concrete base

RIGID LINER Use a glass fibre pond — choose a simple shape (square, rectangle, semi-circle etc) if a surrounding wall is to be built. A thinner polyethylene pre-formed pond may require a wooden frame for support. Colour is a matter of personal preference, but black is the usual choice.

FLEXIBLE LINER Use butyl sheeting — choose a simple shape. A stout wall is required — it will have to take the strain from the weight of water. Make sure that the mortar is set before filling with water. After filling, the edges and corners should be folded and then held down by some form of coping.

NO LINER It is possible to dispense with a liner if the brick or block wall is properly laid on a concrete base. The inside can be rendered with cement to improve the appearance — this is optional but painting the inside with two coats of pond paint is essential. Follow the instructions on the tin.

PLANTING YOUR POND

planting depth

Your pond will need several types of aquatic plants. Water lilies are desirable but not essential in the Conservatory Pond — the requirements are strong light and still water. The main floral effect comes from the marginal plants which usually require to be set at a shallower depth than the dwarf water lilies. With both of these types it is necessary to house the roots and compost in open-sided baskets. Next, you will need oxygenators — these are bought in bunches from the aquatics department of your garden centre. Plant the bunch in a basket of heavy soil covered with gravel — put one basket per sq. metre on the bottom of the pool. Finally there are the floaters which help water lilies to cover the water surface — the roots are submerged but the stems, leaves and flowers (if any) are on or above the surface. Just drop them in the water and remove some as necessary if overcrowding takes place.

Latin Name	Common Name	Planting Depth	Description
WATER LILIES			
NYMPHAEA PYGMAEA ALBA	WHITE DWARF WATER LILY	10 – 20 cm	3 cm wide white starry flowers. Borne freely above purple-backed leaves
NYMPHAEA PYGMAEA HELVOLA	YELLOW DWARF WATER LILY	10 – 20 cm	5 cm wide pale yellow starry flowers. Leaf cover 40 cm x 40 cm
OXYGENATORS			
CALLITRICHE VERNA	WATER STARWORT	See above	Star-shaped leafy rosette on surface. Good in small ponds. Can be temperamental
ELODEA CANADENSIS	CANADIAN PONDWEED	See above	Narrow leaves on long stems. Very efficient but it can be invasive
FLOATERS			
AZOLLA CAROLINIANA	FAIRY MOSS	See above	Dense mats of tiny leaves spread rapidly. Whole surface may be covered
EICHHORNIA CRASSIPES	WATER HYACINTH	See above	Shiny leaves and swollen stems. Orchid-like flowers in well-lit ponds
HYDROCHARIS MORSUS-RANAE	FROG-BIT	See above	Kidney-shaped leaves and small white flowers. Growth is restrained
PISTIA STRATIOTES	WATER LETTUCE	See above	Felted leaves form floating rosettes. Flowers insignificant. Can be difficult
STRATIOTES ALOIDES	WATER SOLDIER	See above	Rosettes of small sword-like leaves come to the surface at flowering time
MARGINALS			
ACORUS GRAMINEUS	JAPANESE RUSH	10 – 15 cm	The variety Variegatus has green and yellow striped leaves. Height 20 cm
CALTHA PALUSTRIS	MARSH MARIGOLD	0 – 5 cm	Buttercup-like flowers appear above heart-shaped leaves in spring. Height 30 cm
CYPERUS VEGETUS	UMBRELLA GRASS	0 – 10 cm	Lance-shaped leaves radiate from the top of the stems. Height 40 cm
HOUTTUYNIA CORDATA	HOUTTUYNIA	5 – 10 cm	Mats of heart-shaped leaves. Variegata has colourful foliage. Height 20 cm
IRIS LAEVIGATA	WATER IRIS	0 – 8 cm	Large flowers — various colours are available. Very popular. Height 60 cm
MENTHA AQUATICA	WATER MINT	0 – 8 cm	Creeping plant used to cover pool edge. Balls of tiny mauve flowers. Height 30 cm
MIMULUS LUTEUS	MONKEY FLOWER	0 – 5 cm	Snapdragon-like red-blotched yellow flowers in summer. Height 20 cm
PELTANDRA VIRGINICA	ARROW ARUM	5 – 15 cm	Deeply ribbed arrow-shaped leaves with arum-like flowers in summer
PONTEDERIA CORDATA	PICKEREL WEED	10 – 15 cm	Heart-shaped leaves with spikes of blue flowers in late summer. Height 60 cm
ZANTEDESCHIA AETHIOPICA	ARUM LILY	5 – 10 cm	Spectacular white trumpets in summer above arrow-shaped leaves. Height 75 cm

THE WATER GARDEN ILLUSTRATED

An excellent indoor water feature — the selection of stone and plants gives this display a natural feel. Unfortunately, it requires a lot of space (and money) to create. ▷

The opposite extreme to the water garden above. No attempt has been made to ◁ *cover the front of the water tank, and this has resulted in the feature having a distinctly unnatural appearance.*

△ *A water garden in miniature. The cascade has been set in the centre of a large container and several pots of flowering plants have been placed around it, with a gravel mulch completing the display.*

CHAPTER 9

PROBLEMS

You cannot expect to look after living things and not have occasional problems. Unlike the artificial house plants which are on sale these days, you are not able to give them a quick dusting and put them back on the shelf. The appearance and survival of your living house plants are affected by your ability to look after their needs, and that is part of the fascination of growing them.

In this chapter there is a detailed look at four common complaints, but there are scores of other problems which may trouble the house plant grower. The first of these other problems arises before the plant gets through the front door. Thinking of the extensive range of garden plants and the wide variety of outdoor containers to be seen at the garden centre, you may be frustrated by the limited range of house plants and the small group of pots, pot holders and containers which are stocked. There are exceptions and things are getting better, but this is of little consolation when the plants and receptacles you want are missing. Some of the varieties you are looking for may be grown from seed, a few may be sold with the outdoor stock, but the only answer for the more unusual plants is to order through an extensive plant directory such as the Plant Finder in the U.K.

Another cause of frustration is the diagnosis provided by textbooks for the common cultural problems. For 'brown leaf tips and edges' the causes listed may be too much sun, water or heat .... and also the opposite extremes, together with dry air and overfeeding! No wonder the cynic must feel "Why can't they just say they don't know?". The cynic is right — the expert doesn't know, and that's because there is not enough information. Your doctor would be in the same position if you went with a headache — he or she could not give you a worthwhile diagnosis. There would be questions to answer such as frequency of headaches, intensity, location, nausea, vision

disturbance etc. And so it is with a cultural plant problem. The house plant textbook gives you *all* the possible causes of a problem — it is then necessary to look at other symptoms to pinpoint the specific problem. Are only the tips and not the edges affected? If so, dry air is almost certainly the cause if the leaves have not been bruised in some way.

In the same way there are a number of factors which cause leaves to drop. Did they fall suddenly without slowly wilting or changing colour? The reason here would be a sudden shock, such as an unusually cold night or the drying out of the roots of a woody plant. If on the other hand some of the lower ones turned yellow and curled before falling, you should suspect overwatering.

All this means that if you have a cultural problem you should use the Plant Troubles section of The House Plant Expert for a list of possible causes and then answer a number of questions to find the specific cause. If a number of plants die prematurely there are other questions to ask — see page 107 for a detailed discussion on this subject.

Lack of sufficient well-lit areas for sun-loving plants is a problem for many people, and it is puzzling for them how plants often look so well in quite shady areas in public buildings. The answer is that the plants don't live there — they just board in these dark corners. The plant servicing company takes them away at regular intervals to recuperate for a week or more. You can do the same thing by moving light-starved plants to a bright spot in a spare bedroom for a week every month.

Finally, pests and diseases. They do occur, but with proper care they are not often a problem. There are sprays, but the decision to use a chemical or not is up to you. Ready-to-use products based on natural fatty acids are available for aphids, mealy bug, scale and red spider, and these products pose no problem for the green indoor gardener.

" WHY DO MY PLANTS NEVER FLOWER AGAIN? "

A flowering house plant is taken home where it blooms quite happily. Nothing wrong with that — it was worth the money and after flowering we either keep it for its foliage or throw it away and replace it with another plant. But then we go to a friend's home and see the same variety in full flower, only to be told that "Oh yes, it's back in flower again". That never happens to us, so what is the secret?

Each plant which is capable of repeat flowering has its own special needs to ensure a further flush of blooms. In nearly every case there are two types of growing conditions. First of all there is a range of warmth, light, watering and feeding for the plants when they are active and in bloom. Next, there is a different range of these factors when the plants are either resting or growing between the flowering periods. With some types such as peace lily this change is reasonably minor — less water and a room which is quite cool are required in winter. But with others the change required during the resting period is more dramatic.

So you can get your plant to bloom again, but you will have to satisfy its particular needs for rest. The rules for individual plants are set out below and on the following pages. Only the popular types of flowering house plants are included here. If your specimen is not listed and it refuses to flower then try the resting technique. Move it to a cool room in a lightly shaded spot and water sparingly for about six weeks. Then transfer it back to its display area and in some cases that should do the trick.

African Violet
You can have several flushes extending over most of the year if you meet this plant's fairly simple requirements. The temperature should be in the 15°–24°C range — above and below are harmful. Use tepid soft water to keep the compost moist and feed with a high potash fertilizer — never a high nitrogen one. Lightly-shaded sunlight is ideal with some strong artificial light nearby when the days are short. A six week rest period is needed in winter — provide a cool room at 15°–18°C and just enough water to avoid wilting.

Azalea

Keep the plant moist and fed after flowering — move the pot to a cool site away from direct sun. Repot into a slightly larger pot using ericaceous compost in late spring. In early summer move the pot outdoors to a partly shaded spot — water and feed to ensure active growth. Bring the pot inside when buds have begun to form in autumn. Keep in a cool room and move to the display area when flowers open.

Bromeliads

The flower-heads on the large, decorative-leaved bromeliads last for months, but when they fade the rosette of leaves at the base begins to die. One or more offsets will be found at the base, and these can be removed for propagation. An alternative is to leave the foliage of the old rosette until it withers — now remove it and put the plant in a well-lit spot, water regularly and feed occasionally. New flower-heads will form, but this will take several years.

Cacti

You have bought a cactus in flower, and you will know that during the spring and summer months it will need watering and occasionally feeding like any other house plant. But it will flower again only if it receives a complete rest in winter. This calls for a shady spot in an unheated but frost-free room with no water during the 3 months of midwinter. When this period is over bring it back slowly to the bright light it needs, and water in increasing amounts until you reach the standard routine in 2–3 weeks.

Christmas Cactus

There are lots of flowers from before Christmas until February but in most cases they never bloom again. The secret is to give them two rest periods before next winter — the first one is for 6–8 weeks after flowering and the second one is from mid-September to mid-November when the flower buds form. This is not the complete rest the desert cacti receive (see above) — a temperature of 10°–15°C is required and so is infrequent watering. Between these two rest periods stand the pots in a shady spot outdoors.

Christmas Cherry

Both christmas cherry and christmas pepper (page 49) are festive favourites, but only the first one can be kept to provide a fresh crop of round berries next year. Cut the stems back once the berries have shrivelled so as to halve the size of the plant. Reduce watering and repot in spring. Stand the pot outdoors in a sunny spot once the danger of frost has passed. Mist the leaves when the starry white flowers appear — pinch stem tips to encourage bushiness. Bring the plants inside before the first frosts.

Clivia

This showy plant flowers every year for some people but not for others. The secret is to give it a period of rest during winter — the two key rules are to give it only enough water to stop it wilting and to give it no fertilizer. It will also help if you can move the pot to an unheated room until spring arrives — you should also refrain from repotting the plant until it starts to push out of the container. Start to water normally when the flower stalk is about 10 cm high.

Cyclamen

The plant will stay in bloom for two months or more in a cool room, but in early spring the flowers will fade and the leaves will begin to wither. It can be kept to bloom again next winter without any difficulty. Stop feeding and gradually reduce watering. In late May put the pot on its side in a shady part of the garden — keep it dry until August and then gradually start to water again. Move the plant to an unheated bright spot indoors until the first flowers form, and then move to the display area. Repot in early autumn every two years.

Geranium

Geraniums have a long flowering period but you may find that they fail to repeat their floral display — this is most likely to happen with the frilly and colourful regal pelargoniums. The reason is that the plants have not been given a winter rest period. The main requirement is to reduce the frequency of watering. You should aim to keep the compost barely moist — do not follow a once-a-week watering plan in winter. Let the surface dry out before watering when in flower.

Orchids

Phalaenopsis and Cambria are the easiest orchids to bring back into flower, but with care all of them can be induced to bloom again. There are no general rules — each one has its own specific needs as described in Chapter 6. There are, however, some general principles. A period of rest is needed in winter or after flowering with the winter-flowering ones — this means cooler conditions and less water for a week or two up to four months depending on the variety. Start normal watering when new growth appears. Some orchids, such as Cymbidium, need a spell outdoors in summer.

Peace Lily

Spathiphyllum with its attractive white flowers has become one of our most popular house plants, and it is a shame that so many of them are thrown away once the blooms have faded. There are three things to do if you want to make sure that your peace lily will produce flowers every spring — use tepid water to keep the compost moist at all times, reduce watering in winter and if possible put it into a cooler room at about 15°–18°C during this resting period.

Poinsettia

It is much easier to buy a new plant next Christmas than to try to save the one which decorated your room this year — bringing a Poinsettia back into flower is a challenge. Cut back the stems to about 10 cm and keep the pot almost dry. Increase watering in May and repot — new shoots will appear. From the end of September put a black polythene bag over the stems from early evening until breakfast time for 8 weeks. From then on you can treat the plant normally — the red-flowered plant will be taller than it was last year.

Rose

Miniature roses are widely available but have never had the appeal of their outdoor big sisters. Two problems are that they lose their leaves in winter, and usually fail to bloom next spring. The way to ensure a floral display every year is to give it a spell outdoors. Repot the plant in autumn and put it in the garden — transfer to an unheated room in February and remove the top half of the stems. After a couple of weeks move the rose back to the display spot where it stood last year.

" EVERYTHING I TOUCH SEEMS TO DIE "

"I am absolutely useless with house plants. Everything I touch seems to die." Talk with a group of people about growing plants indoors and there will always be one who voices this tale of woe. Of course this statement is usually an exaggeration, but there are people who have failed so often that they give up — they just don't have green fingers.

There is no such thing as green fingers. Success is simply a matter of choosing the right plant at the right time and then putting it in the right place and caring for it in the right way. Failing to satisfy one of these four basic requirements will result in poor growth or even the collapse of the plant.

You will have to do some detective work if you are one of the unlucky ones who fails with plants indoors. The death of a single specimen can be due to pest attack or disease infection, but you will have to look for another reason if several types in various parts of the room have succumbed. Go through the following list of possible causes of plant collapse — one of them is the reason for your failures up to now. Correct this mistake and you will have the green fingers you have always envied.

There are some important plant problems which are not likely to be prime suspects in the case of your dying plants. Cold draughts can kill individual plants and so can dry air, but these troubles are unlikely to lead to the death of a varied range of plants. Incorrect watering is the most likely cause but there are other possible reasons which are listed on pages 108–109.

IF ALL ELSE FAILS, GROW CAST-IRON PLANTS

Zebrina

Chlorophytum

There is a group of plants which will tolerate an amazing range of conditions — dreary and cold corners, bright and stuffy rooms, periods of neglect and so on. Grow some of these plants if you are convinced that everything you touch will die. These plants won't, providing you don't keep the compost saturated and you don't bake them on an unshaded south-facing windowsill in summer. Watering should really be based on the particular needs of each plant, but as a general rule you can water once a week during the growing season and once every two weeks in winter.

Asparagus	Fatshedera	Pothos
Aspidistra	Fatsia	Sansevieria
Billbergia	Helxine	Succulents
Chlorophytum	Monstera	Tradescantia
Cissus	Parlour Palm	Zebrina

WHY YOUR PLANTS ARE DYING

You bought pot plants

This is a problem for people whose only involvement with house plants is to buy pots or bowls of flowering plants as an alternative to cut flowers in order to brighten the room. The Chrysanthemum or Cineraria is lovely at first, but the flowers fade and no more are produced. The flowerless plant is unattractive and you throw it away. Actually you have done nothing wrong — these are pot plants which are only temporary residents and even the experts have to throw them away after flowering. If they die after just a few days then you *are* doing something wrong. Make sure there are more buds than flowers when you buy and give it the treatment and position recommended in The House Plant Expert or on the label.

They arrived home in poor condition

This is a possible cause if you always buy from one supplier who is selling poor stock. It may be that the plants are kept in an underlit and overheated spot where the air is dry and watering has been defective. This may be the cause of this condition, but a more likely reason is a basic fault in the way you are taking the plants home. A long journey in the boot of the car on warm days can be fatal, and so can taking the plant from a warm shop into near-freezing weather without ensuring that it is adequately covered.

You bought difficult types

A common problem. Plants are bought without checking the conditions and treatment they require and then they quickly die in the spot you have chosen for them. The reason is that they are in the wrong place and not that you don't have green fingers. Some plants are able to survive and even flourish in a wide range of situations, but some are difficult and need to have their fussy requirements met if they are to succeed. The rule is to avoid plants listed as difficult unless you can give them the position and care they need.

They have been overwatered

This is the commonest cause of a number of different plants dying in a collection. The reason is that very few plants will survive in constantly wet compost, and that means nearly all will die if you are a confirmed overwaterer. Read pages 110–114 slowly and carefully, and then read them again. Apply the basic principles and you may find that you will no longer have to say that everything you touch seems to die.

The compost around the roots has been allowed to dry out

The plant begins to suffer when the compost around the roots is short of water. The first sign of trouble with most plants is that the leaves start to wilt — a warning sign that should not be ignored. Do not confuse with the wilting due to overwatering — see page 111. Watering a dry plant at this stage usually results in total recovery, but with woody plants the situation can be more serious. Here the leaves may fall instead of recovering — this leaf fall is quick and total once the dryness at the roots gets beyond the critical point. Water regularly as instructed — don't expect the plants to recover every time you water after they have wilted. Dryness at the roots is not always due to failing to water the plants often enough. There are three situations where you can water the compost without this water getting to the roots — see 'Water, water, everywhere, nor any drop to drink' on page 114.

They have caught cold

This is a common cause of death of windowsill plants in winter. The curtains are closed on a frosty night and the plants are trapped in this ice-box — the curtains insulate the area from the warmth of the room. Death of the plants is most likely when the room has been kept warm during the day — it is the sudden change of temperature which is so lethal. Move windowsill plants into the room on a cold night if you can.

They have sun-stroke

This is at the other temperature extreme to the problem described above. Once again we are dealing with windowsill plants, but here we have a midsummer condition close to a south-facing window. The effect of the sunlight is intensified by the glass, and the plant is damaged in two ways. The leaves are scorched by the hot sunlight and the roots can be killed by the baking effect on the compost. To avoid trouble in future you should always choose plants described as sun lovers for a south-facing windowsill, and even for these there should be some form of shading against the hot mid-day sun.

You have kept them in the dark

Poor light is one of the major causes of poor flowering and sickly growth, but it is not usually a prime cause of early death. The light-starved plant grows gaunt and weak with pale leaves and few or no flowers. This can go on for months and even years in partial shade — in full shade the plant may succumb much more quickly. The answer is to check the label or The House Plant Expert in order to make sure that the plants you have chosen for a shady site will thrive in a spot well away from a window. There should be a statement that they are suitable for partial shade.

" I JUST CAN'T GET WATERING RIGHT "

Let's face it, watering a varied collection of house plants can be a tricky business. When should I water and how much should I use? Is tap water really suitable? How do I know when a plant needs more water? The list of questions about watering is a long one, and you cannot guess the right answers. There are a number of rules which will help you, but you will need practice as well as book knowledge in order to become skilled in the art of watering.

Watering a plant in a waterproof container is much more difficult than looking after a similar plant in a pot with drainage holes. There is no escape for excess water, and so waterlogged compost is an ever-present threat. If you are not skilled in watering then it is far better to grow your plant in a pot rather than a container.

The proper gap to leave between waterings can vary from a single day to several months — it depends on the plant, pot size, compost, season, room conditions etc. You can get away with a once-a-week routine with a limited number of foliage plants which are listed on page 107, but even here you have to extend the gap between waterings in winter. For other plants you must learn how to tell when the pot needs watering and also the best way to satisfy its need.

There are all sorts of watering aids which are mentioned on page 112 and you may find one or more of them useful, but with experience you should be able to manage with a watering can, your hands, a large bowl and a bucket.

THE FIRST VITAL STEP

If you omit to carry out the first vital step on the road to effective watering then your plant may suffer or even die. It is therefore surprising that this task is not mentioned in the house plant books.

Look at the pot you have just purchased — it is quite likely that the compost surface will be level with or even mounded above the rim of the pot. This makes watering difficult and dryness at the roots can be the result — see page 114.

The first vital step when you buy a plant is to create an adequate watering space. This calls for removing any excess compost in order to leave a gap between the pot rim and the compost surface. This watering space should be about 1 cm in a small pot, 2 cm in a medium-sized pot and 3 cm or more in a large one.

RECOGNISING THE DANGER SIGNS

A plant which has been underwatered can look quite like a plant which has been overwatered.
The floral display is poor and the leaves droop, but there are differences to look for.

Underwatered The wilting of the foliage and the drying up of the flowers usually occur quickly, especially in summer. Growth is stunted. Leaf discoloration may appear over the whole surface, but browning usually takes place along the edges. Oldest leaves fall first. Flowers dry up and may fall.

Overwatered The wilting of the foliage usually occurs slowly or very slowly, especially in summer. When roots rot, however, collapse is sudden. Leaf discoloration may occur over the whole surface, but browning usually occurs at the tips. Both flowers and leaves may become mouldy.

UNDERWATERED   CORRECTLY WATERED   OVERWATERED

Spathiphyllum wallisii

Rosa chinensis minima

Begonia elatior hybrid

LEARN THE RIGHT TIME TO WATER

The test for dryness

There are a number of techniques which can be used to see if a pot or container needs watering.

Tapping Striking the pot with a cotton reel on the end of a stick is an old-established way of telling when it's time to water — the sound changes as the compost dries out. Not recommended.

Lifting A pot can lose half its weight between waterings. A useful spot check, but not the best method. Lift the pot immediately after watering — remember the weight. Lift again when a need for water has been established by another method — again try to remember the weight. Use the span of these weights when you lift the pot in future to see if watering is necessary. Easy for some people, impossible for others.

Store-bought aids Moisture meters and indicator strips are available from garden centres and DIY superstores. Useful on occasions, especially if you are gadget minded. Moisture meters are inaccurate if the mineral content of the compost is high due to the use of very hard water or liberal use of fertilizer.

The finger test The recommended method — see the panel on the right.

The time between waterings

A few plants have unusual needs. There are the ones which need compost which is constantly wet — examples are Cyperus and Azalea. At the other extreme are the cacti which must be kept almost dry throughout the winter months. The air plants need no water at all as they take in moisture through their leaves, and a leafy bromeliad has water poured into its rosette cup. All other plants need to grow in compost which is kept moist but not saturated. Each of these plants falls into one of two groups, and your first job with any plant should be to find out to which group it belongs. Look it up in this book, The House Plant Expert or on the label — you can never be sure you are doing the right thing if you do not have this vital piece of information.

The MOIST/DRY group With these plants the upper surface of the compost is allowed to dry out between waterings — in an average-sized pot this is approximately the top 1 cm of compost. Most foliage house plants belong to this group. The standard technique is to water thoroughly when this drying-out stage is reached between spring and autumn and to water more sparingly in winter. The drying out of the surface between waterings is especially important during the resting period between late autumn and spring.

The MOIST AT ALL TIMES group With these plants the compost is kept moist, but not wet, at all times. Most flowering house plants belong to this group. The standard technique is to water carefully each time the surface becomes dry, but never frequently enough to keep the compost permanently saturated.

Testing an average-sized pot

Inspect the pots every two or three days in summer and weekly during winter.

Rub the surface gently with your finger. If the compost is dry and powdery, water if the plant belongs to the MOIST AT ALL TIMES group.

Insert your index finger to the full length of the fingernail into the compost close to the edge of the pot. If the surface of your finger is dry after it is withdrawn, water if the plant belongs to the MOIST/DRY group.

Problem receptacles

Waterproof containers and large pots can be a problem as the top cm or two may be dry but the compost at the bottom may be waterlogged. A moisture meter is a useful aid here, or you can make a dipstick as described on page 84. When repotting remember to put a layer of grit or gravel at the base of containers and large pots before adding the compost.

LEARN THE RIGHT WAY TO WATER

There are three basic methods of watering, and each one has its advantages and drawbacks. The usual procedure is to use a watering can as the routine technique but to use the immersion method occasionally for some plants and for pots where the compost has become excessively dry. Plunging is employed where the dry compost has moved away from the side of the pot.

The Watering Can method

Water in the morning — droplets on the leaves at night can cause problems such as spotting and rotting. Do not water if bright sunlight is shining directly on the pot. The pot should be stood in a drip tray or in a water-proof pot holder. Pour water slowly into the space above the compost, using a watering can with a long spout. Put the end of the spout under the leaves and close to the rim — let the water drain through and inspect after about 10 minutes. Water again if no water has come through. Empty any water left in the drip tray or pot holder after about 30 minutes. Watering a con-tainer is not so simple — pour in a little at a time and make sure the top layer of compost is not waterlogged. Consider using a moisture meter if you have failed with undrained receptacles in the past.

The Immersion method

A useful technique for hairy-leaved plants such as Saintpaulia and Gloxinia, and also for Cyclamen and other types which do not like water on their crowns. It is also the method to use if the compost has dried out more than usual. Stand the pot in a deep drip tray or a bowl and add water to about one-quarter to three-quarters of the height of the pot. Leave it until the compost surface is wet, which should take 10–30 minutes. Lift out the pot and let it drain — empty the drip tray if one was used or return the pot to its quarters if it was watered in a bowl.

The Plunge method

This is a first-aid technique which is used when the compost has dried out and has shrunk from the side of the pot. Put the pot in a sink or bucket which contains enough water to ensure that the level is above the compost surface. About 5 drops of washing-up liquid should have been added to each litre of water. Put a stone or two on the compost if the pot starts to float. Leave it in the water until bubbles cease to appear — wait a few minutes after they have stopped and then lift out the pot and let it drain. Keep the pot in a cool and semi-shady spot for a day or two if the plant had wilted before plunging.

TYPES OF WATER

Beginners expect the when and how of watering to be a problem, but it comes as a surprise that the water itself can sometimes cause difficulties. There may be things to do with your water if you are growing delicate plants.

Tap water Water straight out of the tap is suitable for most house plants, especially all the hardy old favourites. Cold water can shock the roots of many exotic types, and it is a good idea to let the water stand for a day or more before use. This allows it to reach room temperature — some of the chlorine in the water will disperse during the standing period, but this is not really important. Many experienced house plant growers fill up their watering cans after they have finished and let the water stand for the next watering.

Hard tap water The repeated use of hard water results in a white crust on the compost surface and on the outside of clay pots. This deposit is harmless, but many plants do not like hard water. In most cases the plant can cope with the calcium in the water, but some are positively harmed by hard water. For these plants you should use some form of softened water if you live in a hard-water area. The list of hard water haters includes Camellia, Azalea, Orchids, Hydrangea, Aphelandra, Stephanotis, Brunfelsia and Erica.

Softened water Some types of softened water are safe to use on plants, but others are not. Water from an ordinary domestic unit has been softened by means of salt and is definitely not suitable, but there are several ways to remove or neutralise the lime in hard water. The easiest but not the most effective way is to boil the water and then let it cool and settle, after which the lime-reduced water is used to fill the watering can. Another method of avoiding lime build-up in the soil is to add a teaspoon of vinegar to each litre of water and use this every 1–2 months in place of ordinary tap water.

Distilled water Water from which all the minerals have been removed is, of course, suitable, but bottled distilled water is too expensive to consider. Cost is not a problem if you have a domestic demineralisation unit.

Rainwater A great favourite with keen house plant growers, and it is widely recommended for orchids and other exotics. But do be careful — the water in many open water-butts is polluted and is not fit for use.

WATER, WATER, EVERYWHERE NOR ANY DROP TO DRINK

There are situations where you can be watering regularly, but the compost around the roots is dry enough to cause wilting and even the death of the plant. These troubles are described below — in each case the answer to the problem is very simple.

The surface of the compost has become caked with mineral deposits etc so that water cannot penetrate. The water you pour in to the pot just sits on the surface or pours over the rim.

The answer is to prick over the surface to break up the crust and then to water by the plunge method — see page 113.

At some time the peat-based compost has been allowed to dry out and has shrunk away from the sides of the pot. Subsequent waterings have merely run down this space and out through the drainage holes. The compost will not re-wet with ordinary watering — the answer is to water by the plunge method — see page 113.

The grower has overfilled the pot with compost. Each time you water the compost the surface layer will be wetted, but most of the water will run over the rim of the pot. Watering by immersion will solve the problem, and so will removal of some of the excess compost to create a satisfactory watering space — see page 110.

" THE PLANTS ON MY WINDOWSILL LOOK AWFUL "

It is strange indeed to compare the way we plant up the window box outside the glass and the way we use the windowsill on the inside. Nobody would dream of having a single small plant or a couple of widely-spaced ones in the window box — we fill it with flowers and/or decorative foliage plants to create a miniature garden bed. This is quite different to the average windowsill which carries pots of house plants. It is certainly not a miniature garden feature like its outdoor counterpart — it is merely a base for a pot or two, or perhaps a small container. The plants may well be showing the effect of having been scorched by the sun or chilled by drawn curtains in winter.

It is therefore not surprising that we hear the complaint that the plants on my windowsill look awful. This site is the most popular of all for house plants and there is no reason why it should not be turned into a feature to beautify your room. There are two requirements — you must think about having a plant arrangement rather than a collection of pots, and you must pick varieties which are suitable for the site.

PROBLEMS WITH THE WINDOWSILL GARDEN

• **It blocks the view**
This can be a drawback when the view is attractive. However, an isolated plant rarely improves the view and so it may be a good idea to either have an unobstructed windowsill or to create a windowsill garden which adds colour or interesting shapes to the outside scene. Of course, if the view is unattractive then the windowsill garden's ability to provide privacy is an advantage.

• **It is scorched in summer**
Summer sun can be a problem with a south-facing window, as discussed on page 117. There are four things you can do to lessen the risk of scorch. Choose suitable plants, don't grow them in small plastic pots, provide some shade against midday sun and remember that frequent watering may be necessary.

• **It is chilled in winter**
Drawing the curtains at night can leave the pots in an environment in winter which is too cold for the plants. Moving the pots or containers into the room may be necessary — consider two or more small planters rather than one large one.

ARRANGING THE PLANTS

Your aim is to have a display which is truly attractive and not just a collection of pots with plants in poor condition. To succeed you will have to think of a number of factors before you begin. First of all, the need for shading. A south-facing window will need some form of screen against midsummer sun. This can be net curtains, a venetian blind or a roller blind — failure to provide a screen means that the windowsill is only suitable for cacti, most succulents and perhaps some geraniums. South-east and west-facing windows should also have some form of screening. Next, is the view important? A low arrangement is necessary if it is, but you can be bolder and more dramatic if blocking out the scenery is acceptable or desirable. A narrow windowsill can be a problem — consider placing a table in front of it so as to extend the space available.

The Stand-alone Pot Approach

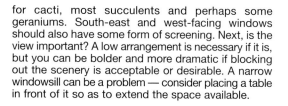

A single Stand-alone Pot (page 66) can provide an attractive windowsill feature, but it has to be in good condition and it should be chosen with care. The reason is that the plant will be a focal point if the window is in a prominent location. A small nondescript plant in a large window will look distinctly out of place, but a large plant in a small window can be an eye-catching feature. A showy flowering plant such as an amaryllis or orchid is a popular choice.

The Pot Group Approach

A single plant can be dramatic, but a group of several plants is generally a better choice if you wish to create a windowsill garden. The classic approach is to have a variety of shapes — one or two eye-catching plants to serve as focal points, several 'filler' plants and a pot or two of trailing types to soften the edge of the sill. This is not a fixed rule — a line of identical plants in designer pots is popular with interior decorators and a line of Sansevieria plants is used in some countries to provide privacy. Whichever style you use, do remember that the pot is a vital part of the display — an odd collection of various materials, shapes and sizes is guaranteed to spoil the display. Stand the pots on a pebble tray (page 79) if you can — the plants will be happier and it will make watering easier.

The Planter Approach

The basic difference between this approach and the Pot Group one is that the plants are housed together in one or more containers (see page 84) rather than in individual pots. With the Pot Group the appearance of the receptacle is important and is often an integral part of the display — with the windowsill Planter it is more usual to choose a plain-looking unit and let the plants provide the interest. Ideally the Planter or Planters should cover most or all of the windowsill — a small Planter on a large sill rarely looks right. Using a single variety as in the illustration can be attractive or you can use the classic approach described above. The herb garden on the kitchen windowsill is the most popular example of the Planter approach.

CHOOSING THE PLANTS

There is no such thing as a windowsill plant — the correct choice depends on the orientation. A variety which can flourish in a south-facing window will suffer from light shortage in a north-facing location. Ivy will do well in a sunless north window but would do badly in the glare of a south-facing window.

Plants for the south-facing window

ACACIA
ANIGOZANTHOS
BEDDING PLANTS
BOUGAINVILLEA
CACTI
CALLISTEMON
CELOSIA
CEROPEGIA
CHLOROPHYTUM
CITRUS
COLEUS
GERANIUM
GERBERA
GYNURA
HELIOTROPIUM

HIBISCUS
HIPPEASTRUM
HYPOCYRTA
IMPATIENS
IRESINE
JASMINUM
KALANCHOE
LANTANA
NERIUM
PASSIFLORA
PELARGONIUM
ROSA
SANSEVIERIA
SUCCULENTS
ZEBRINA

Lobivia hertrichiana

Callistemon citrinus

Plants for the east- and west-facing window

AECHMEA
AGLAONEMA
ANTHURIUM
APHELANDRA
BEGONIA
BELOPERONE
BILLBERGIA
CALADIUM
CALATHEA
CAPSICUM
CHLOROPHYTUM
CHRYSANTHEMUM
COLEUS
CORDYLINE
CROTON

CUPHEA
FICUS ELASTICA
GARDENIA
GYNURA
HOYA
IMPATIENS
NERTERA
POINSETTIA
SAINTPAULIA
SANSEVIERIA
SINNINGIA
SOLANUM
SPATHIPHYLLUM
TRADESCANTIA
ZEBRINA

Chrysanthemum morifolium

Caladium hortulanum

Plants for the north-facing window

AGLAONEMA
ANTHURIUM
ASPARAGUS
AZALEA
BEGONIA REX
BROMELIADS
CHLOROPHYTUM
COLUMNEA
CYCLAMEN
DIEFFENBACHIA
DIZYGOTHECA
DRACAENA
FUCHSIA

GARDEN BULBS
HEDERA
MARANTA
MONSTERA
PEPEROMIA
PHILODENDRON
PILEA
SANSEVIERIA
SCHEFFLERA
SCHLUMBERGERA
SCINDAPSUS
SPATHIPHYLLUM
VINES

Pilea cadierei

Tulipa greigii

CHAPTER 10
HOUSE PLANT MISCELLANY

DARK CORNER DILEMMA

It is a temptation to try to brighten up a dark corner with house plants, but there are questions to ask before you start. Is there enough light? To support any plant it should be possible to read a newspaper in the darkest part in late morning or early afternoon and the plants should cast at least a vague shadow on a bright day.

The test above will reveal whether there is enough light, but you will have to be careful when deciding what to grow. The choice will be limited if the corner is truly shady. In the list below you will find no flowering plants but there are a number of easily-available and attractive foliage ones.

It will help if the surface of the corner is papered or painted in white or a pale colour — a mirrored surface is even more helpful. The list of suitable plants will unfortunately not be enlarged — if you want to have flowers and/or a wider range of foliage plants, it will be necessary to take a different approach. You can use bright-light types for a few weeks and then move them to a bright location to recuperate for a week or two. An alternative route is to buy pots of brightly-coloured flowering types and treat them as a temporary display in the same way as you would treat a vase of cut flowers.

AGLAONEMA	**PELLAEA (Button fern)**
ASPIDISTRA	**PHILODENDRON SCANDENS**
ASPLENIUM (Bird's nest fern)	**(Sweetheart plant)**
FICUS PUMILA (Creeping fig)	**SANSEVIERIA (Snake plant)**
HEDERA (Ivy)	**SCINDAPSUS (Pothos)**
	SYNGONIUM (Goosefoot)

FRUIT BOWL — SAINT or SINNER?

Fruits, such as apples, pears and bananas, emits the gas ethylene during the ripening process. This gas shortens the flowering period of nearby plants, so keep the fruit bowl well away from house plants in bloom. Ethylene production by fruit can be used to your advantage. It will hasten the opening of buds if this is required and it is also claimed that it can help to induce flower formation by bromeliads.

Plants on the windowsill or growing near a window will bend towards the light and the result can be unsightly. The answer is to give the pot a quarter turn every week to ensure even growth — remember to turn always in the same direction.

LUCKY BAMBOO

This age-old Oriental novelty appeared in the shops in the late 1990s and now has become a feature of the displays on offer in garden centres, department stores, gift shops etc. Short green stalks with or without small shoots are grouped together in a decorative container with polished stones or pebbles in the bottom. Alternatively you can buy curled or spiralled stalks of lucky bamboo.

First of all, it is not a bamboo — it is Dracaena sanderiana, which you will find on page 131 of The House Plant Expert. Next, it is grown in water and not compost — the plants should last for years if you change the water every 7–14 days. Do not add fertilizer — use soft water (see page 114) if you want it to last a long time. You can pot up the canes and grow them as ordinary house plants, but the novelty is lost.

Lucky bamboo makes a great gift for Feng Shui devotees, as these plants like all bamboos are claimed to bring health, wealth and happiness to the owner.

More than one third of house plants are purchased because the buyer thinks they will improve air quality. Plants reputed to remove pollutants include Chlorophytum, Dracaena, Spathiphyllum and Ficus.

A simple test for HUMIDITY LEVEL

The atmosphere in a centrally-heated home in midwinter can be as dry as desert air, so it is often useful to know the relative humidity of the rooms where your plants live. You can buy a hygrometer, but the simple guide below will provide you with a quick answer.

Place a tumbler in the refrigerator (not the freezer) overnight. Take it out in the morning and put on a surface away from a radiator or source of steam. Look at the surface after 5 minutes.

Surface frosty at first but it is now clear
The air is dry — most plants will need a moister atmosphere — consider misting, plant grouping, a pebble tray etc.

Surface is frosted
The air is reasonably moist. This is the average situation and most plants should be reasonably happy, although some may need misting.

Surface is frosted — one or more narrow water rivulets have run down the surface
The air is very moist. Nearly all plants should find the air sufficiently moist.

The Survey Scene: OUR FAVOURITE PLANTS

AZALEA

BEGONIA

CACTI & SUCCULENTS

CHLOROPHYTUM (Spider plant)

CYCLAMEN

DIEFFENBACHIA (Dumb cane)

FERNS

FICUS (Weeping fig)

GERANIUM

HEDERA (Ivy)

KALANCHOE

MONSTERA (Swiss cheese plant)

ORCHIDS

PALMS

POINSETTIA

POT CHRYSANTHEMUM

SAINTPAULIA (African violet)

SCINDAPSUS

SPATHIPHYLLUM (Peace lily)

SPRING BULBS

Many plants from the 1990 surveys have kept their place — Christmas favourites such as Azalea, Cyclamen and Poinsettia remain and so do the palms, ferns and ivy. But there have been some quite drastic changes. Orchids were not included in the top 20 in the earlier surveys, but they are now number 3 in the list. The rise of the peace lily is even more surprising, moving from outside the top 20 to number 2. The top spot is held by spring bulbs.

TRANSPLANTING CACTI

Holding a thorny cactus at transplanting time can be a painful job if your hands are not properly protected. Thorn-proof gloves can be used, but a less damaging way is to use a newspaper band. Fold a piece of newspaper to form a 3–6 cm wide band which is quite thick. Make sure it is long enough to form adequate handles when wrapped around the stem and held as shown — gently ease the plant out of the pot and keep it held in this way during the transplanting operation.

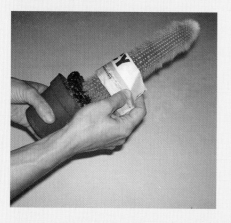

Each year the average European spends nearly five times more on house plants than the average Briton.

The Survey Scene: WHERE WE GROW OUR PLANTS

LOCATION	%
In lots of rooms in the house	34
In one or two rooms in the house	57
At work	22
Nowhere	8

More than 90 per cent of us have at least one house plant at home or at work, and one in three homes have pots in several rooms.

A sharp frost outdoors can result in serious damage to a tender plant in an unheated room. Provide protection by draping a sheet of newspaper over the foliage before going to bed.

BEWARE VINE WEEVIL

You should always look at the soil and roots if a house plant has suddenly collapsed. There will be nothing unusual to see if the cause of death was a shock to the plant's system — an exposure to abnormally cold air or dryness below the critical level around the roots of a woody plant. If the roots are blackened and rotten then you have killed the specimen by overwatering — if the roots have clearly been eaten it is necessary to look in the compost for a 2–3 cm long creamy grub.

This is the larval stage of the vine weevil, and it has become a serious pest of container plants in recent years. The plant and compost should be disposed of immediately, although you might want to take it back to the supplier if the plant was a recent purchase. There are vine weevil-controlling composts and soil drenching materials, but there is little that can be done once the plants have been attacked.

A YELLOW CARD FOR WHITEFLY

Whitefly can be a menace in the conservatory. They can be numerous enough to form a cloud over some ornamentals and they can be persistent enough to be present throughout the year. Unfortunately they are also remarkably resistant to chemical treatment — even regular repeat spraying will not completely eliminate them. A simple control method is to hang up one or more sticky yellow cards which are available from garden centres and DIY superstores. Whiteflies and some other flying insects such as greenflies and thrips are attracted by bright yellow — the surface glue holds them like old-fashioned fly paper.

DECORATIVE MULCHES

You will either love or hate decorative mulches which are placed on top of the compost in pots or other receptacles. They are a popular finishing touch for some designers when creating an indoor plant display — they certainly provide an additional texture and a new colour. It is claimed that they reduce water loss, but this is not a good thing for most plants as this moisture arising from the surface compost increases the air humidity around the leaves.

All sorts of material can be used — coloured glass beads, broken shells, white pebbles, polished stones, grit and dried moss. An exciting and attractive new feature or an offensive and unnatural way of spoiling a display — it is up to you, but before making up your mind you should remember that a surface cover will make the finger test (page 112) more difficult.

Glass mulch

Shell mulch

HANDLE WITH CARE

Very few house plants pose any problems, but it is useful to know which ones can have undesirable effects if eaten or handled.

CACTI.............................. Hooked spines

DATURA .... All parts poisonous

DIEFFENBACHIA .... Poisonous sap

NERIUM .... All parts poisonous

POINSETTIA .... Irritating sap

PRIMULA OBCONICA .... Irritating leaves

SOLANUM CAPSICASTRUM .... Poisonous berries

YUCCA ALOIFOLIA .... Sword-like leaves

The Survey Scene: HOW MANY PLANTS WE BUY

PLANTS BOUGHT EACH YEAR	%
0	2
1 – 4	66
5 – 10	24
more than 10	6

Nearly one in three households buys at least 5 plants every year.

December and March are the top sales months for house plants — the lowest sales months are August, September and November.

Dead flowers and brown leaf tips should be removed promptly — dead plant tissue attracts insects and is a breeding ground for diseases. Shape the cut end of the leaf to copy as far as possible the natural outline of the leaf — unfortunately the browning will generally reappear and a stage will be reached when the leaf should be removed.

In the beginning: AFRICAN VIOLET

The african violet was a late starter. It is one of the world's favourite house plants, but it was unknown until it was discovered in 1892 by Baron Walter von Saint Paul. He found the small purple-flowered plant in German East Africa (now Tanzania) where he was a regional governor, and sent seeds to his father in Germany. The plant was named Saintpaulia in honour of its discoverer, and within a year specimens were being offered for sale in Germany. At the start of the 20th century it was to be found in a number of European countries, but it was not until 1926 that seeds were imported into the U.S. This was the start of the african violet craze — by 1950 there were over 500 varieties in a wide range of shapes, sizes and colours.

CONGO COCKATOO

You won't remember how to spell the latin name (Impatiens niamniamensis), you won't find it in the textbooks and it will not be at your local garden centre. Despite these difficulties it is worth trying to obtain this relative of the simple busy lizzie — there are numerous nurseries which supply it by mail order and you will certainly remember the showy flowers once you have seen them.

The 3 cm long bloom is curved like a parrot beak (hence the common name) and it is gaudily coloured in bright red and deep yellow. Groups of flowers are borne in the leaf axils and the fleshy stems grow at an amazing rate — the usual result after a few months is over-long bare stems with a crown of leaves and flowers at the top.

This is not really a problem. Just cut the stems down to a series of 5–10 cm stubs and they will sprout again — also use the tips of the removed stems as easy-to-root cuttings.

Buy plants which have more buds than open flowers. A good general rule, but there are two exceptions. Choose roses and pot chrysanthemums which are in full flower with very few or no unopened buds.

In the beginning: ORANGES & LEMONS

The story of growing frost-sensitive plants indoors began in Britain in the 16th century with the introduction of the orange tree. Rows of these trees became fashionable in the grand estates in the 17th century, and the large tubs were moved into a "house of defence" between October and April. At first these winter quarters were wooden buildings with few windows and charcoal-burning stoves as shown above. By the 18th and 19th centuries they had developed into the palatial glass orangeries to be seen at stately homes such as Sezincote, Woburn Abbey and Ham House. Sweet and seville oranges were the favourites — lemons were less popular.

Oranges are of course still grown for outdoor display in the summer garden with a winter rest in a conservatory. A popular approach for the house plant grower is to change things over — a dwarf variety such as calamondin orange (Citrofortunella mitis) is housed indoors for its near year-round display of flowers and fruit, with a spell outdoors in summer for fresh air and recuperation. The small fruit on the dwarf bushy tree is too bitter to eat, although it is suitable for making marmalade. The sweet orange (Citrus sinensis) needs greenhouse conditions for fruit production. For fruit you can use when grown under house plant conditions, try the lemon Citrus limon meyeri.

HOUSE PLANTS IN THE VICTORIAN AGE

Towards the end of the 19th century it would have been strange to find a fashionable villa without a Kentia palm in its pot and a variety of green-leaved plants in the parlour. At the start of the century such a display was not a common sight, and there are several reasons for this transformation.

Perhaps the most important stimulus was the rise of the 'middle class' of merchants, bankers and other professionals as a result of the Industrial Revolution. There were both time and money which could be devoted to plant displays in their urban and suburban villas. Next, there was the invention of the Wardian Case described on page 90. This simple idea of growing plants in a glass case meant that plants which could not survive in the smoky atmosphere of the Victorian house could at last adorn their rooms.

'Parlour gardening' now changed from a sideline for the wealthy to a popular hobby for the professional class. Palms and hardy ferns dominated the scene with Aspidistra, Sansevieria, Hedera, Plectranthus etc providing a leafy accompaniment. Plant holders were an important feature — jardinieres, tiered shelves, hanging baskets etc became larger and more ornate as the century advanced. So did the Wardian Cases — simple structures in the 1840s but in the 1860-1890 period they developed into complex multichambered units, hot water-heated chambers, pool-and-plant structures and wardrobe-sized plant cabinets. Ferns were the favourite subject for these cases, but a wide variety of flowering plants and delicate foliage ones were grown.

A de-luxe Wardian Case, complete with ferns and miniature fountain

A succession of books appeared (*Rustic Adornments for Houses of Taste* 1856, *In-door Plants* 1862 etc). Many home and garden magazines contained an indoor gardening column, and so a hobby became a craze.

Conservatories and the smaller window-attached versions (page 93) became increasingly popular after the repeal of the Glass Tax in 1855.

The homes of the wealthy and reasonably well-off became havens for greenery together with Calceolarias, Cinerarias, Begonias, Fuchsias, Heliotropes, Crotons etc, but the position was different in the cottage and working class home. Here pots stood on the windowsill to be near the light and away from the fire, and there was a movement among the reformers of the age to encourage 'window gardening'. The well-heeled gardener was encouraged to 'give material assistance towards the development of a taste which not only contributes to the adornment and beauty of our towns and villages, but to the moral and mental elevation of the dwellers therein ... if flora reigns on the window-sill, order, neatness, and tidiness will pervade all the internal arrangements of the cottage.' (*Thompson's Gardener's Assistant* 1881).

The passion for ornate parlour gardens moved into the 20th century but the steady decline was hastened by World War I. By the 1920s the craze and much of the interest in house plants had gone.

At work in a Victorian conservatory with neither a palm nor an Aspidistra in sight

LIME HATERS

Most house plants prefer water which is lime-free but in general they will tolerate reasonably hard water and a compost which contains lime. However, there are a few types which cannot tolerate lime and so it is necessary to use an ericaceous compost when transplanting and soft water when watering. These lime haters are listed below.

APHELANDRA	**ERICA**
AZALEA	**GARDENIA**
BRUNFELSIA	**HYDRANGEA (blue)**
CAMELLIA	**PLATYCERIUM**
CITRUS MITIS	**STEPHANOTIS**

TRY GARDEN PLANTS INDOORS

There are many plants in the outdoor section of the garden centre which can be grown as house plants. Listed below are ones which are readily available.

AGAPANTHUS	**FERNS**
ASTILBE	**FUCHSIA**
AUCUBA	**GARDEN BULBS**
BEDDING PLANTS	**GERANIUM**
BUXUS	**HEBE**
CALCEOLARIA	**HEDERA**
CALLISTEMON	**HYDRANGEA**
CAMELLIA	**LAURUS**
CELOSIA	**MYRTUS**
CHRYSANTHEMUM	**NANDINA**
COLEUS	**PRIMULA**
EUONYMUS	**VIBURNUM**
FATSIA	**YUCCA**

In the beginning: PEACE LILY

Spathiphyllum wallisii first came to Europe in 1824. It was found by Gustav Wallis in the swampy Colombian jungle — he sent it to various European botanical gardens but it was never again found in the wild. Wallis is remembered in its latin name, but its common names (peace lily and white sails) only came into use when it was developed as a house plant. This glossy-leaved species grows about 40 cm high — once the only type available, but it lost its crown to the larger-flowered and more fragrant variety Mauna Loa. In recent years it is the smaller types such as Gimini which have become great favourites.

SPOTS

There is no single cause for spots on leaves. You should look at the colour and texture of the spots in order to find the reason for the trouble.

Mid brown, dry and crisp — too little water

Dark brown, dry and soft — too much water

White or straw coloured, dry — cold water on leaves or too much sun

Moist and/or sunken — pest or disease damage

POTTED PERFUME

A number of flowering house plants emit a distinct fragrance, ranging from the ones capable of filling a room with their heady aroma (Stephanotis, Lilium auratum etc) to the ones with a much more subtle fragrance (miniature Cyclamen, Exacum etc).

Two words of warning. Perfume is a highly personal thing, so the fragrance you may feel is wonderful may be unpleasant or even overpowering for your visitor. In addition it is usually unwise to have two or more scented plants growing close to each other. Despite these cautionary points the pleasant aroma of scented flowers is generally a welcome bonus and some suggestions are given below.

CITRUS	**JASMINUM POLYANTHUM**
CONVALLARIA	**LILIUM (some)**
CYTISUS CANARIENSIS	**MANDEVILLA**
DATURA	**NARCISSUS (some)**
EUCHARIS	**NERIUM**
FREESIA	**OLEANDER**
GARDENIA	**ORCHID (some)**
HOYA	**PLUMARIA**
HYACINTH	**SPATHIPHYLLUM**
IRIS RETICULATA	**STEPHANOTIS**

POTTED HISTORY

The use of house plants to decorate rooms and hallways became a popular craze in the 19th century (see page 124), but the house plant story is much older. It is known that plants were grown in pots by the Egyptians, Romans, Greeks and Chinese well before the birth of Christ, and it is assumed that many of these pots stood indoors. It could be that pots of herbs or garden flowers have stood on windowsills from time immemorial, but the story of growing exotics indoors really starts with the crusaders and then sailors bringing back specimens from the East in the 13th–15th century.

In the 17th and 18th century the aristocracy throughout Europe had their 'plant houses' with coal braziers or hot-air heaters for their oranges and other exotics, and in 1653 the first book to discuss gardening indoors (*The Garden of Eden*) appeared. Plants began to appear in the parlours of the wealthy, but the idea of using plants to furnish ordinary homes did not really take hold until the 1850s.

The first half of the 20th century was a quiet time for house plants. Between the wars there was little enthusiasm for filling the living room with all sorts of ironwork, pots and plants — few new plants or new ideas appeared. The end of World War II saw a renewed interest in indoor plants as harmful gas was replaced by electricity and central heating, and a flood of new varieties appeared.

Indoor plants in the 18th century home